THE SOURCE STUDY

PATRICE HUNT

WESTBOW
PRESS®
A DIVISION OF THOMAS NELSON
& ZONDERVAN

WestBow Press books may be ordered through booksellers or by contacting:

WestBow Press
A Division of Thomas Nelson & Zondervan
1663 Liberty Drive
Bloomington, IN 47403
www.westbowpress.com
844-714-3454

ISBN: 979-8-3850-0653-3 (sc)
ISBN: 979-8-3850-0654-0 (e)

Library of Congress Control Number: 2023916748

Print information available on the last page.

WestBow Press rev. date: 09/12/2023

I dedicate this book to

Roderick W. Russell

You were the first person I gave a copy of my completed
manuscript to. I just wish you were here to hold the fruition
of this work of obedience in your hands. Even though you are
gone I want you to know your prayer has been answered.

"I pray for the day that the width of my shoulders will become
as strong as the wind you've been beneath my wings."

Roderick Wade Russell
Seven Pillars of a Prosperous Life

ACKNOWLEDGMENTS

To my supportive, loving, and wonderful husband Marcus. There are so many more adjectives I could use not only to express who you are to me but who you are as a man. Growing with you in love and life all these years, has been amazing. However, what makes me love and respect you more has been having the opportunities to grow with you in faith. Your confidence in, and obedience to God are inspiring. I thank God every day that I get to do life with you.

To my three beautiful children. I hope that you know how much joy you have brought into my life. Even during the chaos and hard parts of life, the three of you have been the best blessings from God. You are honestly three of the funniest people I know. I pray that if you learn nothing else from me that you learn to love God and keep him as your source.

To my friend Kisha, you are so many things to me. God uses you to speak to and encourage me so much that I feel every time we talk on the phone, He is on three-way. LOL I am inspired by your obedience to him and his will for your life. I know that there is so much that he wants to do with and through you and I am enjoying watching from the sidelines.

To my Granny, Mrs. Shirley D. Russell. Yours is the voice in my head, there is not a day that I don't quote something you say. I honestly believe that what Papa told you about Harris' is true. Without you I don't know where or what I would be. You have shaped me in so many ways, especially in my faith. It was under your tutelage that I came to have a relationship with God. I am grateful that I was able to be raised by you, and my Pawpaw.

Finally, to my parents, aunts, siblings, family, and friends. Thank you all for your never-ending support and encouragement. I know that God truly has placed each and every one of you in my life for a reason. I pray God's continued blessing over you all.

FORWARD

There are two instances in the bible where God used a rock to provide water to the Israelites when they were in the wilderness. The first is Exodus 17:1-7 and the other is Numbers 20:2-12. In Exodus when the Israelites complained about not having water, God told Moses to take his staff and HIT the rock at Horeb and water would come out of it. However, in Numbers God told Moses and Aaron to take the staff and SPEAK to the rock and then the water would come out of it. But that is not what they did. Instead, Moses hit the rock twice with the staff. God took this act of disobedience as a representation of Moses' lack of trust in Him. As punishment God told Moses that he would not get to lead the people into the promised land. In both instances the Israelites were in need of water, and in both instances, God provided them with water. However, in Exodus Moses was obedient and in Numbers he was not.

While writing this book there were a couple of times when I went for days and maybe even a week where I didn't write anything. One time in particular there was three weeks to a month where I only wrote one or two days during that entire time. One morning, during that time God placed these two scriptures on my heart. He revealed these two scriptures to remind me of Moses' disobedience. Moses hit the rock when he was supposed to speak to the rock. Yes, the water still came out and the people's thirst was still quenched. But that was because God had already put water in that rock. It was always apart of God's plan to use that rock to provide water for the Israelites. God was not going to let Moses' disobedience keep him from blessing his people they way he had already planned.

There is something in this book that is meant to minister to or encourage someone. It is a part of God's plan to use what he has instructed me to write to bless someone. God put this book in me for a reason, so that he may be glorified and that someone may receive what he has for them through this study. I may never know who it is for, and I may never know what impact it will have. But it is my job to be obedient. If I follow Moses and HIT the rock instead of SPEAK to it as instructed, then I can miss my opportunity to receive my blessing that is attached to this act of obedience. This book that you now hold in your hand is my submission to God and his will for my life and this book. May it bless and encourage everyone who reads it, and may God be glorified in it.

CONTENTS

CHAPTER ONE

THE SOURCE

GOD is the source! OK now that that's out in the open we can get to the good part, the understanding of it all. God placed this on my heart so many years ago I don't even remember when it was or how he did it. All I know is that he spoke this into me as a Bible study and I started jotting down experiences, making notes, looking up scripture, definitions etc. Then nothing, for years this sat in the back of a notebook that I looked at about once a week but never turned the page to see it. Then finally in 2021 something started stirring. I wanted more than anything to hear from God the way I once did. You see I use to hear from God all the time. Not like a booming thundering voice from the heavens. But more like a thought dropped right into my spirit that I could not shake no matter what until I did what he was leading me to do. I was diligent, obedient, and totally reliant upon him when we first started our reciprocal relationship (you know the one where it wasn't just him pursuing me, but I pursued him also and allowed myself to be fully in relationship with him) It was all so new. Our intimacy was palpable, everything about it excited me. I looked forward to our time together and could and did spend hours reading, praying, and worshipping. But somewhere along the way it changed. Slowly, spending time with him changed from something I was blessed to do, into an item to check off on my daily To Do List. Sure, I would hear from him occasionally. He would give me Nuggets of wisdom, but it wasn't the same. The intimacy wasn't there. I knew what the problem was, it was me. I had let everything else in my life take precedence over my most important relationship. I mean I was still going to church and Bible study (virtual bible study but bible study still the same) I was still reading devotionals and spending time in my prayer closet every morning. But I just didn't feel that connection, that closeness that I had once grown accustomed to. I had just started going through the motions. Maybe This is why he placed this on my heart again. Not so that I could put pen to pad to share with someone else. But so that I, myself can reconnect to him, my source.

I reached out to my friend/ prayer warrior/ confidant/ mentor in the faith and sometimes spiritual adviser, Kisha Robertson. (She has a great podcast called Ruth Speaks) I called just to check in and catch up. I decided to share the news that God had placed on my heart to write this Bible study. (At the time I didn't know what it was going to be but more to come on that) Her response was one that I could expect from Kisha based on who she is in my life. It boiled down to something like, about time I knew it was coming. To know her is to know that she was being completely honest. God had probably shared this with her two days after we met which was seven years before this conversation took place. She is just one of those people who has that type of connection with God. But some other things she said in that conversation struck a chord with me. The first was, why can't it be both. Her response to me telling her that I didn't know whether this was meant to be a book or a Bible study. The other thing she said was your thorn is your ministry. It's the constant thing or struggle that you have to deal with. That thing that God uses to minister to others through you that keeps you on your knees and sometimes prostrate on your face. If we were in a cartoon that's when the light bulb would have turned on above my head. Was the subject of God being the source one that he placed on my heart to delve into deeper because in my own life I was struggling with relying on him to consistently be my permanent source?

My husband is the breadwinner of our household. He owns his own business. Just when we purchased a new house, we went through a drought that lasted more than six months with no income. He had done the work, but the client didn't pay. The mortgage was due, and our resources were gone. My mind and past experiences with God reminded me that he has never failed us. But there is a part of me that remembers that time when it seemed to me, he had failed me. We had been married for two years and had a 7-month-old baby girl for whom I had quit my job to be a full time stay at home mom. Right then, that's when my husband lost his job. Oh, and did I mention we had just moved into a house from an apartment because we needed more space and wanted a nice backyard for our baby girl to play in. He had a degree and had never had a problem getting a job so initially we didn't think much of it. We still went to church every Sunday and prayed and believed God for a job. We lived off his severance package, unemployment, and a Lone Star card until that ran out too. After two years and eight months of having to live with my parents and then his parents, God answered our prayers. No, he did not fail me. But he sure did take his sweet time. If I'm honest in the beginning, it felt like he was failing me. My relationship with him grew through that experience though. I got closer to him and learned to depend on him as my source, hear his voice, and follow his lead. But that didn't change the fact that for two years and eight months my husband couldn't find a job, and neither could I for that matter. We had to live in other people's houses. We got our car repossessed. Nothing we had was earned by our own hands. Instead, it was given to us by people that God had placed in our lives to bless us. And if I'm honest I wasn't afraid that God wouldn't provide for us this time. I was just afraid that he would choose to do it in that same way.

You see it's easy to faithfully see God as my one and only source when it's a flowing river. But that doubt starts to creep in when that flowing river turns to a dripping faucet. As Christians we always quote the scripture that God's ways are not our ways and his thoughts are not our thoughts, which is totally and biblically true. But sometimes that quote has more legs to stand on when you are quoting it to someone else about their situation than when we are quoting it to ourselves about our own. I am one of those people that can say I have tried him for myself, and I've seen him work. But sometimes I wish he would work how I want him to when I want him to. When I'm going through my situations and circumstances with faith and hope keeping an eye out to see his hand at work along the way, I wonder why not now? I have been trusting and believing you for this all the way up to this point. Why not just fix it now?

I wonder if Abraham felt that way. He trusted that God would provide a sacrifice in Isaac's place. And he could have at any time: at the foot of the mountain, while they were climbing the mountain, while they were preparing the altar, or lighting the fire. But no, God did it in the 11th hour. There was Abraham knife in hand about to sacrifice his son for whom he had prayed. And that's when God provided the literal ram in the Bush.

I truly believe that God waits to act, so that we can exercise our faith and more so our trust in him. Will we stay the course? Will we believe in him and what he has promised us against all odds and the voices surrounding us. This world has so many pitfalls and problems sat out for us, and God knows about and has provided us a way through them all. But we must get to that provision.

I imagine there being a map of my life with God as the map maker. He knows where it begins and ends. He knows all the landmarks, mountains, and valleys. Because of that he puts in rest stops and gas stations. He puts them in the perfect spots because he knows where on this journey, I am going to get tired and when I will need to be refueled. Through this life when my eyes start to get heavy, or my gas light comes on I have to trust God and keep driving knowing that he has placed everything I need on my path at the right point in time. Even if it seems like it's the 11th hour. I have to trust that he won't allow me to fall asleep before I make it to that rest stop or that I won't run out of gas before I make it to his station. I have to trust that he is truly my omniscience source.

Merriam Webster defines source in multiple ways. We will cover some of these definitions and prayerfully by the time you get to the end, the Holy Spirit will have revealed the Lord to you in each one.

The first definition of Source is a place, person, or thing from which something comes or can be obtained. This definition can be shown in two ways; originate and derive.

When a person or object originates from something or somewhere it's the point from which it comes. I originate or came from Galveston TX, born and raised. However, I no longer live there. But I must say that there are things about myself that I know are the way they are because of where I come from. I think I have a hurricane 6th sense, meaning I can sense when I need to leave or when it will be OK to stay. There have been times when everyone else has fled from a storm and I knew we would be fine if we stayed, so we did. There's a saying about BOI's. (People born on islands) They are said to have salt water in their veins. So maybe this is why I feel that I can predict when it's best to stay and when we need to go.

I love water, it calms me. It can be an ocean, river, lake, pool, or even the rain. Another thing is something that I have done since childhood. I wear flip flops everywhere and to everything. I will put on a pair of flip flops no matter the season or occasion. They are my most consistent shoe selection whether in June or December. My feet and flip flops are kindred spirit. I am sure these and other things are ingrained in me because of where I originate from.

The same can be said about my family dynamic and upbringing. My grandparents raised me and because of that I am an old soul. Early to bed, early to rise, no matter how hard I try I just can't lay in bed past 10 AM. There are so many traditions and beliefs that I hold onto to this day because of who raised me and where I come from. I know these traits about my personality are there because of my point of origin. Because of my source.

The other part of this definition, derive, is when something is taken especially from a specified source specifically. That's a lot of specialness in one definition. Another synonym for derive could be obtained which is to get, acquire, or secure something. Nutrients can be derived, confidence can be derived, words and languages can all be derived. One example is raspberries, they are the best fruit source from which to derive fiber. Meaning your body can obtain a good amount of fiber from the raspberries you eat. There is fiber in other fruit of course but at 8 grams per serving, they are high in soluble fiber.

Usually when you see the word derived it is followed by the word from, derived from. That is because you are tracing something from its source of origin. In essence it is the act of taking or receiving something from its source of origin. You can also use derived when you can see parts of the original in something. You can say that baseball was derived from cricket. There are similarities between the two sports even though they are different. Both have pitchers, umpires, batters as well as bats. (Even though they look different) The French language is said to be derived from Latin and even though it is distinguishable enough from Latin to be deemed its own language you can still hear its Latin origin in many words.

The biggest difference between originate and derived is that yes, I originate from Galveston. But you cannot go back to Galveston and expect to see me still there because, even though that is where I came from, it is no longer where I live. However, when something is derived from something or someplace it is a continual source for that particular thing. Using my Raspberry examples for instance. Knowing they are a good source of fiber; you know you can always get fiber from a Raspberry. When something is derived from something else it is also possible to see the source of origin in the product that was derived from it.

The next definition for source that we will talk about is a spring or fountain head from which a river or stream issues. A spring is a naturally occurring source of water. It forms when water pressure causes groundwater to flow onto the earth's surface. There is water under the ground and when it rains it puts pressure on that water and that pressure forces the water to flow to the surface through the cracks and tunnels in the surface. There you have it a spring is formed. Springs fall into one of three categories: perennial, intermittent, or periodic. Perennial means that the spring is constantly flowing all year long. Intermittent is a spring that is only active after it rains or during changes in the season.

Lastly periodic springs such as geysers vent and erupt at intervals that can be irregular or regular. Each of these types of springs can be an example of how God demonstrates his presence as the source in our lives. He is constantly there all the time. A source for us to draw from, consistently sustaining us. But he can also be found when the pressures of life rain down so heavily on us that we need him to saturate the dry spaces in our life. And yet still there are times when we need him to erupt forcefully onto the scene producing a right now miracle.

The last definition for a source we will look at is a book or document used to provide evidence in research. While writing this book I've had to research different things, such as the definition of source, what a spring is, as well as what fruits are good sources of fiber. I couldn't just make up this information and stick it in this book. I had to find real factual trustworthy authorities to get this information from. Once I found the information, I couldn't just use it as if it was my own, I had to credit the person or website that I received the information from. In other words, I had to find a reliable and honest source from which to attain the communication of the information I was seeking.

There you have it, the four ways we will use to look at God as our source.

1. Source of Origin
2. Source of Derivation
3. Source of Fresh Water
4. Source of Communication

In three of these four ways we see the Holy Trinity. God the father is our source of origin, where we come from. God the son is our source of derivation, where we obtain our salvation. God the Holy Spirit is our source of communication. God speaks to our hearts through the Holy Spirit and the Holy Spirit speaks to God on our behalf as well. I would like to elaborate a little on each of these three as well as God as our source of fresh water.

SOURCE OF ORIGIN

First, our source of origin, where we come from. When we look back in Genesis 2:7-8, 18, 20-22 we can clearly see that God is the source of origin for all mankind. In Genesis 2:7 we can see that he made man from the soil and in vs 8 we see that he breathed the breath of life into man. Further down in verse 22 we see that God made woman from man's rib.

We are both physical as well as spiritual beings. You know that we are physical beings because God made us from the soil where the trees and grass grow which like our physical bodies will someday waste away. But then he did something different. Something he didn't do for the trees or grass or even the animals for that matter. He breathed the breath of life into us. He gave of himself so that we would exist. I believe that piece of him that he gave us, is what will one day rejoin him in eternity. Like it says in 2 Corinthians 1: 22 it's a deposit guaranteeing what is to come. That is God's spirit within us. His indwelling spirit is the trait that is distinctive of where we originate from, God. It's like my storm 6th sense or love of water and flip flops, but oh so much better. You see that which God breathed into mankind is our soul. It's connected to him; it longs to rejoin him and to be in relation with him. Since God is our source of origin there are traits that we have that are a nod to him. God made us in his image. Genesis 1: 26 tells us that he gave us authority over everything else he created. Animals survive off instincts, but God gave us a mind to understand, reason, create, etc. Therefore, we should not be controlled by our wants and sinful desires. But instead, we should exercise our authority, abilities, and self-control that are byproducts of our origin, the almighty God. Even his words are powerful.

God created the heavens and the earth and everything therein just by speaking it all into existence. Because we originated from him our words also possess power. Proverbs 18: 21 tells us that the power of life and death are in the tongue, but we must be careful how we use it. We have received all this because of our source of origin. But what are we going to do with it?

SOURCE OF DERIVATION

Next our source of derivation, God the Son, or Jesus Christ. Jesus is where we receive our salvation. Before God sent his son the people had to make sacrifices multiple times a year for sins, atonement, trespasses, etc. Oh, but God! We see in Philippians 2:7-8 that Jesus being found in appearance as a man humbled himself and was obedient to death, even death on a cross. Why, you may ask. Why would God the Son, part of the Holy Trinity humble himself, put on human form just to suffer and die a humiliating death. Well Isaiah told us why hundreds of years before it ever even happened. In chapter 53 verse 5. For us! It was for us, he was wounded for our transgressions, bruised for our iniquities, he bore the punishment for our peace. It is because of all this that we are healed. What makes this even more amazing is that God the father raised him from the dead and seated him on his right side where he intercedes on our behalf (Romans 8: 34). All that we must do to be saved is confess with our mouths that Jesus is Lord and believe in our hearts that God raised him from the dead. By doing this the results will be salvation (Romans 10: 9 – 10). This is proof that we derive our salvation from Jesus, and just like you can always go to raspberries when you need fiber you can always go to Jesus if you are in need of salvation. And because God the father is our source of origin and our source of salvation is derived from God the son, we should be able to see parts of him in us. That which should be indiscernible between him, and US is the fruit of the spirit found in Galatians 5: 22. Those traits that come through because of our source of origin and from which our salvation is derived.

SOURCE OF COMMUNICATION

The third source, our source of communication. Represents the Holy Spirit. God speaks to us, as well as leads and guides us through the Holy Spirit. Luke 12: 11-12 tells us that we don't have to worry about what we should say because the Holy Spirit will be our source and teach us at that time what to say. I can honestly say that the Holy Spirit has been my complete source for this book. I never know what I'm going to write when I sit down. He will just put something on my heart to say and I will listen, obey, and write it down. There is yet to be a time when I have sat down and had absolutely nothing to write. Every time I submit to his will and sit down with my notebook and pencil (yes, I am handwriting this LOL) he gives me the words he wants me to say. I know he is using this to speak to my heart and I pray to yours as well. I could not have come up with half of what he has given me for this book. This whole experience is Matthew 10:20 being carried out in my life. For it is not you who speaks, but it is the spirit of your father who speaks in you.

The most astounding thing about the Holy Spirit being our source of communication is it goes both ways. Not only can he communicate what we need to know or do, but we can also communicate with him. The books, websites, and dictionaries I used to find the facts for this book gave me information but that's all they could do. I can't open a book and ask it for a better explanation because I didn't quite get the meaning behind what it was trying to convey. I can't ask it how I should go about doing what it suggested I do. Well, I could but it definitely would not give me an answer. The Holy Spirit however not only gives us clarity when we ask for it, he also intercedes on our behalf with the father, It tells us so in Romans 8: 26-27.

We actually have someone who knows us fully, knows God the father fully, and knows God's will for us fully. Who goes to God on our behalf, not haphazardly but according to the will of God. How blessed are we! He is like our prayer cheat code (it's the up, up, down, down, left, right, left right BA, start of prayer. I may have just dated myself with that reference but if you played video games in the mid to late 80s you know)

The same Holy Spirit who speaks to us today is the same spirit that spoke to the prophets and apostles in the Bible days. Just like he gave them the words to say and write all those years ago. He will give us the words to say and write as well. We can trust what they wrote because

2 Timothy 3: 16 tells us all scripture is God breathed and is useful for teaching, rebuking, correcting, and training in righteousness.

SOURCE OF FRESHWATER

Lastly our source of freshwater. Like it says in Genesis 2: 5-6 before God sent any rain, he allowed streams to come up from the ground and watered the earth. He used the stream or the surface water to prepare the ground before he made any grass, plants and I am taking creative liberty to include trees in that as well. So, I am going to say our source of surface water is God's provision for us. Sometimes we feel weighed down by the pressures of trials, tribulations, circumstances, and situations. We feel like everything is raining down on us at once, nonstop. It is in those times that pressure forces God's provisions to the surface.

When we were buying our house, we had a situation with one late payment from a year before. It was threatening to bring our home buying process to a complete halt. But God. When the pressure of that situation started to rain down on us, he provided a spring. A spring in the form of a Christian woman that worked at the company. She did what needed to be done not in the seven days she said she would try to do it, but instead in 24 hours which made the monthly cutoff date so that it would be reported to the credit bureaus that same month.

There are so many other situations like this. Situations when I felt like I could not lift my head because of the pelting from the rain pouring down on me. And you know what happened each and every time. Just like surface water, God's provisions sprung forth. Flooding my life with his unmerited favor.

Questions

1. Before we really begin to dive in. Would you classify God as your source?

2. Share some traits you possess that are indicative of your origin.

3. Given that we all derive our salvation from Jesus Christ. Do you feel there is evidence in your life of that fact?

4. Read Isaiah 53:1-12. How does reading that passage of scripture make you feel?

5. Has there been a time in your life that you felt the Holy Spirit placing something on your heart to do? Did you do it?

6. Can you recall a situation where God demonstrated himself as your surface water?

7. Can you think of a time when you have experienced God's unmerited favor?

Chapter Notes

CHAPTER 2

THE TREES AND VINE BRANCHES

There are many instances in the Bible where God refers to us as trees. Jeremiah 17: 7- 8 being one of them. He refers to us saying blessed are those who trust in the Lord, whose confidence is in him. They will be like a tree planted by the water... Or maybe Isaiah 60: 21 when he says your people will live right and always own the land; they are the trees I planted to bring praise to me (CEV). The same sentiment is conveyed in Psalms 1: 3, Ezekiel 42: 12, Psalms 92: 12- 14, and Psalms 104: 16. We are trees.

I try to run at least three miles three days a week. I take the same route because I am a creature of habit. On this run there is a huge tree by a lake that is towering and reminds me of Jeremiah 17: 7- 8. One day I went for a run after listening to a meditation where that scripture was quoted and suddenly that tree became the natural representation of that scripture. To see it towering above the house next to it with branches spread wide. I know that tree doesn't fear the Texas heat or worry about the February freeze to come. I know in early March that tree doesn't doubt whether its leaves will return in spring. That tree is literally planted by its source. It is immovable, it is steadfast, it is strong. I want to be that tree. Confident in my existence because I am aware of my proximity to my source. Speaking of confidence, I once heard the difference between confidence and trust explained in such a way that it has stuck with me ever since. The best way I can interpret it is to just say that trust is believing in something when you have no evidence. While confidence, on the other hand, is having assurance based on experience. Early on in my Christian walk I trusted God. I believed that he would and could get me through something even though I had not yet opened my eyes to His working in my life. However, now I have seen him bring me through so many things so many times in so many unbelievable ways. I now have evidence. I have past experiences, tangible real-life results to back up that trust. So now I should be that tree, I should be confident in my source because he has sustained me time and time again. Because he has never failed me even if he didn't go about it the way I thought he would in the time frame I thought he should. I need not fear, doubt, or worry. I should be as confident as that tree planted by the lake because like it says in Hebrews 13: 8 Jesus Christ is the same yesterday and today and forever. And if he is the same that means I can expect the same results, maybe not the same execution but the same results. Which is him ultimately working all things out for my good. And if I can expect the same results I should be as confident as that tree that I see next to that lake.

In drafting this book, I learned a lot about trees, a lot more than just the parts of a tree diagram coloring page they gave us in first grade with the leaves, trunks, and roots pointed out. I learned about how a tree functions. Now just because the tree is planted next to the lake doesn't change the fact that it is still a tree in this world and must go through the seasons like every other tree. Its leaves will not always be green. One day its branches will be bare. It is the same with us, we are going to have to go through changes, experiences, and even losses. We will inevitably have fall and winter in our lives but the thing to remember is all that we can see happening externally to that tree is a representation of what is going on internally. You see in fall its leaves change colors not because it's pretty or to let us know it's time for Thanksgiving, but instead because of a lack. In the fall months the days are shorter and therefore trees get less direct sunlight. With the decrease in sunlight the chlorophyll in the leaves starts to break down. Leaves use chlorophyll to absorb the light from the sun and transform it into sugar for energy and food for the tree. Chlorophyll is green so the green color of the leaves is a by-product of the chlorophyll within them. Because of the decrease in sunlight the leaves are no longer using the chlorophyll for what it was intended, therefore it ceases to exist. It is a supply and demand thing. When the demand decreases so does the supply. With the lack of chlorophyll, the leaves are no longer green and that which already exists but lies beneath the surface is now able to be seen. The orange, burgundy, and yellow colors of the leaves that we see in the fall were always there but not previously visible because of the more dominant green color from the chlorophyll.

Sometimes God will use the seasons of lack in our lives to allow our true colors to come through as well. We may lose a job, mate, or even a friend. Through that loss it will be revealed to us that we were placing our hopes and faith in that job, paycheck, or relationship. If we really look at ourselves as trees, the leaves are that external part of us that others see. Not just our outward appearance, but our persona, personality, character, and lifestyle as well. The green leaves represent the times in life when things are going well. There is no perceived lack. We have everything we need and probably some of the things we want. But sometimes if we are not diligent during these "green leaf" times we can forget who is really sustaining us. We can start to prioritize things and people over our relationship with God. We can take him and all he does for us for granted. We can feel like we got ourselves to where we are. That our hard work and intelligence are what made us successful. Or maybe we allow our joy to be wrapped up in a spouse, friend, child, even a car or house. We do like it says in Romans 1: 25 we exchanged a truth about God for a lie. We worship and serve created things rather than the creator. We find it easier to forego Bible study to take our kids to dance on Wednesday nights. We miss church on Sunday morning so we can work in the yard, wash the car, or work around the house. We stopped doing our daily morning devotions to lay in bed and cuddle with that special someone just a little longer. No, I am not saying any of these actions are sins, none of them are even bad in and of themselves. They can even be described as well meaning. But one day we look up and we have good intention God right to the sidelines of our lives. We thank him before we eat. Say goodnight before bed, we may even send up a quick prayer request. But there is no intimacy, no desire to be close to him or hear from him. Then BAM fall comes. And in this season with the decrease in chlorophyll our true colors start to show as the green fades away. Something happens and we realize that which was lost had become an idol and had slowly but surely replaced God for the top spot in our lives and now that it is gone, we are left scrambling with the exposed yellows and oranges of life.

WINTER

Oh, but Fall is not the end, it is just the beginning. We all must go through winters. You see leaves are important to sustaining a tree, but they are fragile. Remember our leaves are our personality, persona, character, and lifestyle. That is all fragile too. Leaves wouldn't survive the winter and if a tree tried to hold on to their leaves during the winter the tree would be susceptible to damage. So, what the tree does is it takes as much nutrients as it can get from the leaves, then it forms a protective barrier between the leaves and its branches. Because the leaves can no longer give and receive from the branch they fall off. You see leaves excrete excess water and the tree knows that in winter the ground freezes making it harder for the roots to absorb water from the soil. Therefore, there will be no excess water to sustain the leaves. So, the tree strips down to just that which is necessary so that it can be sustained during the harsh winter months. And that is what happens to us. We must let go of caring about what other people think of us. We must rely on God and not ourselves, other people, or things. We must be all in, bear, willingly being sustained by our one true source.

VINES

I can see how in our individual relationships with God we are trees. It centers around us as the trees and God as the source. A tree is self-contained. It has many parts, but it grows up and independent of the trees that surround it. When we are talking about vines however, there is one central trunk that all the branches spread out from. Though they go out from the main part in many different directions, they are still each connected to the vine. As a part of the body of Christ we are the branches on the vine. And God, he's the keeper of the vineyard.

My dad has a vegetable garden in his backyard. He grows different greens, cantaloupe, cucumbers, okra, and more. He was going on vacation for about 2 weeks in the middle of a very hot summer. His garden needed to be tended while he was away. I volunteered to go over and do what I could to help out. Truth be told I would describe myself as having a black thumb. I have killed even the hardiest of plants. But since I know how important the garden is to my dad I went over a couple of days in the evening and watered his garden. However, I had my own plans, and we took the kids out of town for a few days. When I came back, I went over to water it again. But this time some of the leaves on the cantaloupe bush were turning brown and the leaves on the other vegetable bushes were wilting. I did what I could, but I am no match for my dad. You see he tends to his garden while I just went over and watered it once a day. My dad waters it once in the morning and once in the evenings. He pulls off the dead leaves and picks the ripe vegetables to promote growth. He pulls weeds and makes sure his enclosure is secure so nothing gets in to eat away at his crop before he can harvest it. My dad is a loving and committed keeper of his garden. That is the way God tends to us. He takes care of the vineyard, knowing what to do and when to do it. He knows what's best. But the difference between my dad and God is that God doesn't go on vacation, he doesn't take a break. He never leaves us in the hands of another or to our own devices. If we stay connected to the vine, God, the vineyard keeper will tend to us.

In the New Testament Jesus used the example of branches on a vine to describe his relationship with us. In John 15: 5 he says he is the vine, and we are the branches and if we stay joined to him, he will stay joined to us and we will produce lots of fruits (CEV). But without him we can do nothing. The branches are the part that the fruit and leaves grow on. However, a branch cannot survive on its own. It must be connected to something; it must be connected to the Vine. If we believe the word, it tells us that Jesus is the one true vine. As branches we get our nourishment and support from the vine. As Christians each of us branches out from Jesus and we all play our part and have the same job to do. We are all to bear fruit. The good thing about this is we do not have to do it alone. We get everything we need as branches from the vine, while the vineyard keeper (God) provides the perfect conditions for us to be fruitful.

This analogy reminds me of 1 Corinthians 12: 27 where it tells us that we each represent a part of Christ body. Our job as a part of the body of Christ and as a part of the vineyard are the same. To disciple others or "Bear fruit." We are all connected but if I get so caught up focusing on the branches next to me, I will not be able to effectively do my part and my fruit will not grow. If I don't do the one thing I am called to do, which is bear fruit then I am ineffective. If I am ineffective then the vineyard keeper has no choice but to do what it says in John 15: 2.

LEAVES

In order for me to be an effective fruit bear I must stay connected to the vine. Once I am sure that I am connected to the vine then my leaves need to be appealing. My leaves need to look like Jesus leaves. I told you leaves serve a purpose. They are important and present on vine branches as well as trees. As I said when we talked about the trees, our leaves are our persona, personality, character, and lifestyle. These all need to mimic Jesus. We need to have love for others and be outward focused. No one wants to hear what you have to say just because you claim to be a Christian. You must earn your right to be a part of someone's life before you can fully disciple them. Oftentimes it is our leaves that do all the talking without us even knowing. People will see you from afar and take notice of how you react to different situations, your joy, kindness, compassion, love for God and others, and it will make them want to know what sustains you. It's not just in Spring and summer months when you leaves are green either. People who are a part of your life and know what you have going on see when the seasons of your life change from summer to fall and even winter. They notice how you handle those times. Whether you lose hope or hold on to it. They also notice where your hope comes from. They see that despite the change in your circumstances your belief and confidence in God remains the same. And for some people it is not what you say but how you live in the good times and the bad that draws them to God.

Jesus touched the whole person, and we should as well. When he preached to the multitude in Matthew 15: 32- 37 and it got late and people got hungry, he did not say OK peace be unto you, bye, to be continued. He met their needs, he fed them, and not just spiritually. When Jesus was teaching in Luke 5: 17- 25 and the men lowered their friend down through the roof he did not say I'll pray for you and keep right on teaching and preaching. He healed him right there on the spot. When Jesus was teaching in the synagogue in Luke 6 and the man with the paralyzed hand was there, he did not ignore his need and keep sharing the gospel with the rest of the crowd, he healed him as well. You see God will place people in our path that we are to do more than just pray for. We are to be his hands and feet, we are to do something for them, help them in some way. Then, once that need is met, they are in a better position to receive the gospel we have to share. You see bearing fruit is arduous work. It's not all pretty leaves just to reel them in, there must be something there to help sustain the growth.

When we are saplings, new shoots on the vine, in other words new to the faith we need encouragement and to be poured into. As young Christians we need to be nurtured. The enemy wants us to fail, he wants us back no matter the cost. Those that are more mature in the faith have the duty as our brothers or sisters in Christ to support and to be there for us, so we won't fail. Vine branches often have tendrils that grow out from them. The point of the tendril is to attach the vine branch to its support. You see, because of the way vines grow they need support, or they will crawl along the ground like watermelon vines. Crawling is fine for watermelons but not for grapevines. Without a support to climb, the fruit will sprawl across the ground and rot because the branch is not strong enough to support itself. This is why the vineyard keeper provides a support system. So, the vine branches will attach its tendrils to the support and climb. Climbing is a learned behavior; some types of vines don't climb by habit they have to be taught how to do this. But once taught they can climb with the best of them. We are born into a broken, fallen world and our sinful human nature is what comes naturally. We naturally want to crawl along the ground because it's easy. But God requires that we strive toward the image of Jesus, this is a learned behavior. We must choose this day who we will serve as it says in Joshua 24: 15. Once we make the decision that, as for me and my house, we will serve the Lord, then we need mentors in the faith, a support system. We need fellow believers that we can spiral ourselves around like tendrils on a trellis so that they can do what it says in Hebrews 10: 24 to spur us on toward love and good deeds. That is why the next verse is so important, verse 25 tells us not to give up meeting together. We are branches on a vine, the body of Christ, part of a whole. We are not made to do life alone, we need each other. We need fellowship! You see the thing about tendrils is they respond to physical touch. Once they feel an object is suitable for support, they coil around and grasp onto it. We were made to do life together in relationship, no matter how you look at it. As branches we need to remember that we are all a part of, and connected to, the one true vine, Jesus Christ. As trees we need to remember who our source is and the importance of staying connected!

Questions

1. *Read psalms 1: 3, Ezekiel 42: 12, psalms 92: 12- 14, and psalms 104: 16*

2. *Based on the explanation given in the text, do you feel you have confidence in God or trust in him?*

3. *What green leaf times have you been blessed to experience?*

    a. *Was there an Autumn or Winter that followed. If so, reflect on what God taught you through that Season.*

    b. *What season are you in now?*

4. *Do you honestly believe the statement that God works all things out for your good? Why or why not?*

5. *Read Jon 15:2 What will God do to us if we are unfruitful? What does that mean to you?*

6. *What is the difference between us as trees and us as branches?*

7. *Do you have a support system in the faith that does what it says in Hebrews 10:24? Are you that support system for someone else?*

Chapter Notes

CHAPTER THREE

THE WATER

If we are the trees and vine branches in this analogy, then what is God. Well, he is the water. As I stated in the previous chapter, He is also the Vinyard keeper. There are so many different scriptures in the Bible in which God uses the analogy of water (him) being the source for trees (us). But why? What is so amazing about water that it makes it such a great example of God's place in our lives? Well, everyone can understand and relate to it for one thing. The importance of water is known around the world. Water is timeless. It is as important to human life today as it was back in Genesis when God created man and animals.

Another important thing to note about water is that it has been here since the beginning of time, literally. In Genesis 1: 1-2 it says that the earth was formless and empty, darkness covered the surface of the [*watery depths*]. Which means before he created anything else: sun, moon, or trees, there was water. So, it is no accident that the metaphor he gives us to represent himself as the source of our lives is the literal source of all life. I also find it interesting that he didn't give it all to us at once. In verses 6-8 of the same chapter, it tells us he separated the water above from the water below. This leads me to postulate that he puts some on reserve for those times we need him to rain down on and completely saturate us.

As I explained in Chapter 1, a spring can be formed when it rains, and the water enters the aquifer (a body of permeable rock that can contain groundwater) and puts pressure on the groundwater already there. This pressure forces the water out of that aquifer and up to the surface through cracks in the surface. The groundwater was always there under the surface, but it wasn't until a little pressure was applied that it revealed itself. Like I said before when we are feeling the pressure of life falling down on us, it is in those times that God uses that pressure to naturally reveal himself to us. The pressures of life forces us to allow God to come to the surface.

I want to go a little deeper into three different categories of Springs. Perennial, intermittent, and periodic. A perennial spring is constantly flowing, all the time. An intermittent spring is what I described above. Only active after it rains and during changes in seasons. A periodic spring erupts at intervals that can be regular or irregular. Remember, Geysers are periodic springs. I want to say a little more about how these three different types of springs are also indicative of three different ways, God sustains us. He is always there for us as a perennial spring. A constant source on whom we can depend no matter what's going on. We can rely on him. We know where he is and that he will always be there. But there are sometimes when we go through seasons where we feel bogged down and heavy. It is in those times that he is an intermittent spring. He uses the pressure that we feel, to seep through the cracks and fulfill our need for peace, hope, joy, and most of all, Him. Then there are the times when there is nothing left to do, nowhere left to go. There seems to be no hope for our situation. That is when like a geyser He erupts into our lives creating miracles and strengthening and sustaining us past what we thought was even possible. Making ways where there seemed to be no way. The one thing these three categories have in common is that they are all springs. Whether they're constant, Intermittent, or erupting, all three are sustaining Sources.

God has always been there and will always be there for us. We can walk beside him, allowing him to be the constant in our lives. He is also within us just under the surface nourishing us and quenching our thirst. But don't discount when things get particularly heavy, and we need him to do more, to be more, when we need a downright miracle because it feels like everything, and everyone is against us. That is when he will spring forth his presence. Where there was once dry ground now there is water. There is a song we use to sing at vacation Bible school that says, I've got a river of life flowing out of me. Makes the lame to walk and the blind to see. Open prison doors set the captives free. I've got a river of life flowing out of me. Spring up a well within my soul, spring up a well and make me whole. Spring up a well and give to me, that life abundantly.

Water is important for many reasons, one of which is that we as humans need it to survive. According to the Mayo Clinic, as adults up to 60% of our body is made of water. The interesting fact is that as a baby 78% of your body is made-up of water. Which leads me to draw the conclusion, the more immature you are the more water you need. How true that is in life and this analogy. 1 Peter 2: 2 states God wants us to be thirsty like newborn babies (CEV). The younger we are in our faith the more we need God to show us that he is our source. We don't have confidence in him due to the fact that we lack the experience of having gone through something and seen how he brought us through.

Another interesting thing about the use of water to represent the source, is how we view it. When we have water, we waste it. I can't tell you how many times I have gone around my house picking up half full bottles of water. Then instead of finishing that bottle, the next time the culprit is thirsty they go get another one. Or how often I hear the shower running and the person that is supposed to be taking a shower, is instead walking around distracted wasting the water. However, when water is scarce, when there is a lack of water or it is not easily available to you, you understand its importance. You will do whatever you have to, to get it because you understand that it is integral to your survival.

In some parts of Africa and Asia women and children walk an average of 3.3 miles just to get water. Risking severe damage to their neck and spine due to the heavy loads of water they must carry on their heads such long distances. Most times the water is not even clean and clear. It's often the same water the wildlife drink and bathe in. Do you think, if they had the bottles of fresh clean clear spring water available to us, they would leave them half full for days on a nightstand just to get another one because it's no longer cold. Do you think they would dance around their room listening to their favorite station on Pandora while that warm clear clean water gushes down the drain never to return?

The reality of water fits the analogy of water. Those of us who have it readily accessible take it for granted. While those of us for which it is truly deficient cherish it with all our hearts. God as the water in our lives also gets taken for granted. We coast along in life reaping the benefits of the many blessings of God. We have a roof over our heads, clothes on our backs, food on our tables. And every day we allow ourselves to be lulled into a false sense of security that what we have, we deserve or have earned of our own accord. The further away we get from the lack and the deeper we get into the fulfillment, the more we forget God. Then one day, the diagnosis, a layoff, a loss, a betrayal, and we don't know what to do. We have wandered so far away from our source that we can no longer just drink him in through our roots.

While I was looking into the many uses of water, I came across the website www.theimportantsite.com, it listed the top 10 reasons water is important to us as humans. I believe there is a spiritual component to each of the reasons listed on the website. I've taken the liberty of listing the reasons from the website with my own Spiritual explanation.

1. WATER KEEPS OUR BODIES HEALTHY.

Our organs need water to work properly. It protects the organs and tissues of our body. It carries nutrients and oxygen to our cells, lubricates our joints, and helps our kidneys and liver functions by flushing out waste. We all know that without water our bodies become dehydrated. Dehydration can be defined as a harmful reduction in the amount of water in the body. When we are dehydrated our mouths and lips become dry, we feel tired, dizzy, and our bodily functions don't work properly. The same can be said when we are spiritually dehydrated. Our speech is dry, we don't have anything good or uplifting to say. Because we are not casting our cares on God and instead trying to remedy them ourselves, we are tired and rundown from trying to carry everything on our own shoulders. We are dizzy, (which is defined as an altered sense of balance or place) because without God leading us we have no direction on where to go next and no real grasp on where we are now. As I stated earlier, we need water (God) to function properly and without it (Him) not only are we not able to reach our full Godly potential, but it also becomes increasingly difficult to carry out our daily responsibilities.

2. WATER PREVENTS FATIGUE.

Water boosts our energy levels. Because we are vessels, we pour out God into the lives of those we encounter. If we keep pouring and pouring without ever being replenished, we will have a lack and be thirsty. We will find ourselves demonstrating some of the symptoms of fatigue in our Christian lives. We start to focus on all that we are doing for others with no reciprocity, and we become moody and irritable. Without God as our burden bearer, we get weak from trying to carry our problems and the problems of those around us. Because we try to fix everything on our own, we have impaired decision making and judgment when we find nothing we try makes it better. But that is not what God intended for us. He says in John 4: 14 that whoever drinks the water he gives will never thirst (nor be fatigued) because that water will become a spring of water welling up to eternal life. In keeping God as our source, we are able to pour into the lives of others he puts in our path freely because when we are rooted and planted in Him, we have the ability to drink him in anytime from the spring within.

3. WATER IS NECESSARY FOR WASHING AND SANITIZING.

We were filthy because of our sins. We were unclean because of our iniquities. But Jesus Christ loved us so much that he tells us in Ephesians 5: 25-27 that he gave himself up for us to make us holy. Cleansing us by the washing with water through the word and to present us to himself radiant, without stain or wrinkle or any other blemish but holy and blameless.

4. & 5. WATER IS USED TO GROW AND RAISE FOOD.

We use water to raise crops as well as livestock to feed people all over the world. As I said in #2, we are vessels that God uses to pour himself into the lives of those we encounter. As he uses us to pour himself into the lives of others, they grow spiritually because they are being spiritually nourished. Just like crops grow when they are being watered, we grow as well. We are called to do what it says in Colossians 1: 9-10 which paraphrased says to continually pray for others and ask God to fill them with knowledge and wisdom and understanding. So, we should basically intercede on behalf of others. A lack of water can devastate crops, dehydrate, and starve livestock, which then would result in a famine. When there is a lack and we don't allow God to use us to pour into the lives of those he places in our path, they won't have what they need to grow, and this can produce a drought in their lives and cause them to fail. As I said in chapter two, we are to bear fruit and if our fruit fails, then we are ineffective.

6. WE USE WATER TO PREPARE FOOD.

We boil, steam, and rehydrate. Water is needed to prepare many types of food. Through prayer and meditation, he prepares us to receive our spiritual food which is the word of God. He doesn't just prepare the spiritual food, but he also prepares our hearts and minds to receive the food. Psalms 10: 17 in the King James Version tells us that he will prepare our heart. When we go to God in prayer, it puts us in the right mindset to receive that which he is trying to feed us.

7. WATER CAN BE USED TO PRODUCE ELECTRICITY.

Fuel, natural gas, oil, and uranium all take huge amounts of water to produce the energy we use in our day-to-day lives. In John 9: 5 Jesus tells us he is the light of the world. There are numerous other verses where he is described as the light as well. The Lord is my light and salvation Psalms 27: 1. I am the light of the world whoever follows me will never walk in darkness John 8: 12. The true light that gives light to everyone was coming into the world John 1: 9. Just as water is used in producing the energy we need to light our everyday lives. Jesus, the light of the world, produces the energy to light our souls.

8. WATER IS AN IMPORTANT PART OF MEDICINE.

Water is used to clean medical tools, equipment, as well as the hands of doctors and surgeons. Only things that have been cleaned or washed can safely enter the sterile field. People's hearts are broken, their minds are ailing, and God wants to use us as he makes them whole again. But if we have not been cleansed, sanitized, and washed as in #3 then we are not fit to enter the sterile field to be used by God to save that person's soul. We are to be the hands and the feet of God so that he can use us to save the sick. But if we ourselves are contaminated we will only make things worse.

9. CLEAN WATER PREVENTS FATAL DISEASES.

If you drink water from an unclean source, you can contract dangerous diseases like cholera and typhoid fever which could ultimately lead to death. This is why <u>clean</u> water is so important. Sometimes in our Christian walk we try to allow other things to be our source. It's not the pure clean water of God but it is something different. It is contaminated. Contaminated with lies, selfishness, criticisms, envy, judgment, self-satisfaction, and self-reliance. Everything wet isn't water and just because it temporarily quenches your thirst it doesn't mean it's going to satisfy and sustain you. What is the fatal disease that drinking from this contaminated source can cause, sinfulness. It tells us in Romans 6: 23 for the wages of sin is death but the gift of God is eternal life in Christ Jesus our Lord. So, you can choose to drink from the contaminated source that ultimately leads to the grave or you can choose the clean pure living water which leads to eternal life.

10. WATER IS A HUMAN RIGHT.

We all need water to survive, and we all have a right to clean safe water. It is the same with Jesus. He died so that we may all have a right to him, to the salvation that he so freely gives. We need it not only to receive eternal life, but we need it for our spirit to survive this life as well. It too gives us hope and a future as it says in Jeremiah 29 :11. A relationship with God is not just for the elite or people with unlimited resources. A relationship with God is free and available to anyone who wants it because of the sacrifice Jesus made on the cross. All we have to do is confess with our mouth that Jesus is Lord and believe in our heart that God raised him from the dead. And receive our water. He is waiting.

All ten of those reasons, are great examples of why God is important as our source. So why is it so hard for us to accept him as such? Jeremiah 2: 13. Says my people have committed two sins. They have forsaken me, the spring of living water and have dug their own cisterns, broken cisterns that cannot hold water. What God is saying in this scripture is that we have turned our backs on him. Instead of using him as our source, we try to be or create our own source to sustain ourselves. We feel like if we get a good enough education then a high enough paying job and find that perfect spouse and have those perfect kids that everything in life will work out the way we want it to. That we will be living our #bestlives, being our #bestself and nothing will ever go wrong. We think our money can sustain us. We think our title or relationship status can sustain us; we think our position in the Community can sustain us. But the interesting thing is that I can no more sustain myself than I can water my flowers with Soda. It is scientifically proven that you cannot use any other liquid but water to grow plants. The molecules in water are shaped differently from the molecules in other liquids. Because they're shaped differently it blocks the process of photosynthesis from happening. Without the process of photosynthesis, the seeds don't get the message that they should be growing, so they don't. Therefore, when we try to sustain ourselves with earthly accolades, we look as silly as someone trying to water their flower bed with Gatorade. Or maybe we don't try to be our own source completely. But instead, we try to contain him and compartmentalize him into different parts of our lives. We say okay God, you can have my attitude and I'll be nice to people, but I'm going to take care of my finances myself. Or, you can have my marriage, and I'll put you first in that. But I'm going to take care of my career and ambitions myself. That is not what God wants. God wants to be Lord over our whole lives. He wants to be our source and sustain us in our entirety. He wants to use us in the operating room, courtroom, the classroom, our house, our car, in Walmart, and in Target. He wants us to allow him to be our source 100%. Without any limitations.

Questions

1. Read 1Peter 2:1-3. What is God telling us through this scripture?

2. Do you think you have ever taken God for granted? Explain.

3. Have you experienced God as your perennial spring?

4. Give an example of God sustaining you in these two ways?

    a. Intermittent.

    b. Periodic.

5. Have you ever felt spiritually dehydrated?

6. Has there ever been a time in your life that you can recall trying to have something or someone other than God as your source?

7. Have you ever tried to compartmentalize God in your life? If so, what was the result?

Chapter Notes

CHAPTER FOUR

THE DISCONNECTION

It has been established that God is our source. We understand that in this analogy we are the trees and vine branches, and God is the living water. What else do we need to know? What is left to say? Well, now it's time to dig a little deeper. If God is our source what happens when we sever that connection? You notice I didn't say what happens when we become disconnected from the source. That is because God is always available to us. He loves us and desires to always and forever be our source. So, if we are not connected, it is not by accident or happenstance but instead because of a choice we made. Not because He turned his back on us but because we turned our back on Him.

The fact of the matter is, it's not always one big choice that we make that disconnects us. Sometimes it is a combination of small, seemingly insignificant choices that pushes us further and further away from God. I imagine we all can come up with scenarios in our minds that we think would describe the lives of people who are disconnected from God as their source. Take a moment to think about it, what would that person's life look like? A person who is no longer connected to God as their source. I would wager to guess that each of us would have imagined someone whose life wouldn't look so good from the outside: struggle, lack, discord, they would be visibly downtrodden. Their life would be a wreck. That may very well be the case for some, but not necessarily for all. How many of us would imagine a suburban wife and mother that is on the PTO and volunteers at her church. Maybe a seemingly successful businessman, doctor, or lawyer who is a great father and provider. Or how about the teenager that goes to church, seems to love his or her family, have their "head on straight", babysits the neighborhood kids, is a star athlete and or an honor student. Because of what the world deems as "good" and "successful" I bet none of us would think these people fit the scenarios that we came up with. I know they did not fit the ones I would have come up with before. Before what you ask? Before I disconnected.

The funny thing is, during that time I would not have classified myself as disconnected. I was doing all the "things" I should. Checking all the religious boxes but leaving all the relationship ones unfilled. And all that time I never realized that I had walked away from God as my source. I still believed that he was my savior. I still believed in heaven and that Jesus died was buried and rose on the third day for the forgiveness of my sins. I still prayed from time to time read my Bible and went to church. I acted the part and definitely looked the part depending on who was looking. I did everything I thought I was supposed to do. Everything people expected "good" Christians to do. The problem was not my actions. No, the problem was the lack of heart behind the actions. The problem was my motives. I was not doing all these things to cultivate or pursue a relationship with God. I was doing all these things because they were what I was "supposed" to do. I was doing them so that I could feel like, and other people would think that I had everything together. It wasn't until I needed him to step in that I recognized my thirst and realized that he was missing in my life.

I love to travel, and I enjoy seeing the different sights staying in different places but there's nothing like home. You know when you go on vacation, you're so relaxed and happy to be away and you feel like you could stay there forever. But, as it gets closer and closer to the end of your trip, you start to miss the creature comforts of home. I know for a fact that I have said "I can't wait to get back to my bed" while still on vacation. For you it might not be your bed. For you it may be your couch, your shower, your big TV, or something altogether different. It's not until you have gone a while without it that you realize how much it means to you and therefore start to miss it. It wasn't until I turned to drink from my source that I realized I had wandered too far away for my roots to absorb the water. As I journeyed back to God. I took inventory of the little compromises I made. The times I chose my way versus Gods way. The times I rationalized action and decisions that did not quite line up with God's will for my life. That's when I realized I missed his peace, his joy, his guidance, and his overall presence in my life.

The great thing about our God is the freedom we have. The bad part about us is that we don't always exercise that freedom in the way that He desires us to. God gives us free will so that we will choose him. We were not created as mindless drones. He is not going to force himself on us. On the contrary he will wait patiently for us to realize that we need him and his love. As it says in 1 Timothy 2: 4, He wants all people to be saved and to come to the knowledge of the truth. But we can't think that coming to the knowledge of the truth is the end. Because it is just the beginning.

Once we come to believe, then we have an opportunity for a relationship. We have access to the water, and the freedom to drink freely of it. There is a difference between having water and drinking water. My son will tell me he is thirsty and ask for a juice box. My response is usually "it's not Juicebox time but you can have some water." I estimate that 75% of the time he will walk out of the kitchen, no juice box, and no water either. Now did he just want juice or was he not yet thirsty enough to take the water I was offering. The other 25% of the time I know he is actually thirsty because there will be no further discussion. He will get his cup and drink the water. Water was present in both scenarios but in only one was his thirst quenched. How many of us as Christ followers are choosing to remain thirsty because what God is offering doesn't look or taste like what we had in mind.

A big difference between life and the above example is that as the mom I can offer water and if it's not taken, he goes upstairs still thirsty. However, in life when what we want looks different than what God is offering at the time, the deceiver often presents us with an alternative offer that looks and taste like what we desired. The problem with that is drinking contaminated water leads to disease. Remember? Eve fell into this same trap. God made fruit from every tree in the garden of Eden available to her, except for one. What did the serpent do? He slithered in and tempted her with the one fruit she couldn't have. When she succumbed to the temptation and took that bite Eve traded her intimacy with God for a piece of fruit. The glaring red flag in this story is Eve's lack of trust. She didn't trust that what God told her was true, nor did she trust that he had her best interest at heart. When we find our backs up against a wall or in any type of situation the most important decision we must make is whether to trust God or ourselves.

As I shared at the start of this book there was a time that our family was going through a financial struggle that went on for months. I can honestly say that at that time it was a daily battle going on between my spirit and my flesh. Do I trust God or worry, do I stay the course or try it my own way? As I said before this wasn't the first time that we had been faced with this type of situation. My friend Keisha and I have talked about the concept of being spiritually fatigued. I would describe this as a struggle with something or some situation for an extended amount of time. Or being faced with the same struggle repeatedly. (If you remember the quote from earlier "your thorn is often your ministry".) When this happens, you get tired of enduring, praying, and believing when there seems to be no noticeable change in circumstances. Or when the same issues continually reared their ugly heads. Spiritual fatigue can lead to becoming disenchanted, which can lead to becoming disconnected and once you are disconnected you can't hear his voice or feel his presence. If you can't hear him or feel him then where does your encouragement and hope come from and without hope you can't have faith. So, you see being disconnected can lead down a slippery slope that can end in a pit that is very hard to climb out of.

My husband and I have faced hard times and God has always been there for us. Though it has not been easy he has provided for us and guided us by strengthening our faith and solidifying our relationship with him. That, however, doesn't keep the thoughts at bay. I still get tempted to try to find a way to fix things myself. Should I try to get a job? Should I go to this person or that person? I still want to manage it, to speed up the process. But I know he knows what's best for me because he can see the past, present, and future. So, he knows what needs to be done in the grand scheme of things. I trust him; I trust that he knows what's best for me and that he is working things out for my good. I had confidence that there was going to be a solution to that situation just like there has always been in every situation before. Even though some of those solutions were not what I thought or may have wanted them to be at the time.

Whenever I come back to my senses after having a woe is me pity party about how hard my life is and why God has not fixed my current situation. I think of the Israelites in Exodus 15: 22-24. Now three days after leaving the Red Sea; (you know the one that God parted allowing them to walk through on dry land, then used to drown the Egyptian army that was charging after them.) Yes, that Red Sea. The Israelites were in the desert and could not find water and when they did, it was undrinkable. So, what did they do? They did what some of us do, or what all of us may have done a time or two. They started to complain and then they questioned Moses about what they were going to drink. Now you mean to tell me that you just witnessed God part a whole sea so that you can walk through it and then used it to defeat your enemies and you're going to doubt, whether THAT God can provide water for you. How? But the interesting thing about this is I have done the same thing. God has worked downright miracles in my life and the next time I come to a little bitter water I somehow miraculously forget the Red Sea he just parted. I have seen him work in my life and the lives of my family and friends. I have seen him put people in positions to bless me and my family. I have seen him cure diseases. I have seen him heal sicknesses. I have seen him mend relationships. So why is my memory so short when I get to my next hurdle?

A common misconception is that once we accept Christ as our savior our life will be smooth sailing. But just like a tree (even one planted by a lake) has to go through all four seasons every year of its life. We too must face the seasons of ours. This is not our home, so looking for perfection here is futile. Being connected to God as our source doesn't absolve us from any difficulties in life. But it does ensure that we have someone by our side and on our side that is powerful and willing to go on this journey with us. Someone that knew this difficulty was coming, and ultimately works all things out for our good. Even if it doesn't seem that way in the beginning.

I don't know about you, but I often find it easier to see God as my source during the difficult times. When I need his encouragement and hope to get through the day. Those are the times I absorb him in the most. I go to him in prayer and seek his comfort and guidance constantly. Therefore, it should come as no surprise that it was not in a season of lack that I found myself disconnected. No, instead it was in a season of abundance. Why is it that when God blesses us, we forget him. Hosea 10:1 gives us a great example of this. Israel was prosperous, and the richer the people got the more they worshipped idols. I am going to make this about me, because I don't know how you react, but I know what I have been guilty of doing myself. Why is it that I push God to the back burner of my life once he has given me what I asked for. Why does my comfort make me lazy and lackadaisical in my pursuit of God.

If you remember our leaves are the external part of us that others see. Leaves on a tree absorb water. But it is not a highly effective way for a tree to receive the water it needs because leaves also excrete water. The best way for a tree to receive its water is through its roots. A tree couldn't survive if its only source of water was through leaf absorption. This reminds me of a day I went over to my neighbor Shondra's house for coffee. I noticed Spirit, her peace Lily plant. (Yes, she names her plants as all good plant parents do I guess). Spirit's leaves were drooping and turning yellow. I asked Shondra what was wrong with Spirit, she told me that she needed water, and she needed to be repotted into a bigger planter. A few days later I went over again for coffee and noticed that Spirit was thriving again, and she was in a new pot. With this new pot there was a hole you poured the water in at the bottom and the pot kept the excess water on reserved for when Spirit needed it. When she brought the new pot Shondra also bought a misting spray bottle to mist Spirits leaves. This helps increase humidity around the plant. However, the misting of the leaves is a complement to the water on reserve in the pot that is being absorbed through spirits roots not a substitute for it.

As I said before our leaves are our persona, personality, lifestyle, and character. Now when we are connected to the source leaves can be beneficial to fruit bearing. However, when we are disconnected, they can inhibit fruit growth. Leaves are the part of me that others see, parts that I use energy to form and maintain but they don't produce fruit. The leaves job is to make food for the tree or vine branches through photosynthesis. They also provide a little shade to protect the fruit from harsh heat. But leaves need nourishment to grow as well. What happens when we use all that we have to make leaves? There is no nourishment left for fruit growth. Matthew 21: 18-19 talks about a time when Jesus was hungry and saw a fig tree by the road. He went up to the tree expecting to get a fig to satisfy his hunger. Instead, he found nothing except leaves. Our lives can be like this tree. We can look full and flourishing but upon further inspection you will see that we are only full of leaves. When we are in our season of abundance there can be a temptation to put all, we have into leaf production. We post on social media; we buy and do things that make us look and feel good. We live our #bestlife. We make sure to walk the walk and talk the talk, but it is just lip service. We are just living life for the gram. We hold the opinion of others so high that we put more stock in who they think we are than who God created us to be.

We know that God is our provider. We know that all we have comes from him. But it seems the more leaves we have, the easier it is to forget what it feels like to be thirsty. To forget that we need to be in close proximity to him to drink him in through our roots. We start to believe that what we have we deserve or have earned. We forget what James 1: 17 tells us, that every good and perfect gift is from above. Instead, we start to believe that our success is of our own doing, and we become prideful. We become arrogant and start to believe that we are self-sufficient. If we are self-sufficient, then what do we need God for? If we can sustain ourselves then there is no need for any other source.

Another way of living that demonstrates being disconnected from the source is living a double life. I have also been guilty of this one, especially in college. Living a double life is when you try to live worldly part-time and godly part time. Even though that is not possible. What is most amazing about this is the lack of self-awareness that it's happening, in real time. I would hang tough with my friends on Friday and Saturday nights doing all types of things that did not line up with trying to live like a child of the King. Then on Sunday morning I would drag myself out of bed to go to church like I was doing God a favor. Or I would be on the yard speaking in a way that is more representative of a sailor as they say, than a child of God. Then that night, go to choir practice with the Baptist Student Movement and use that same mouth to sing praises to God. There were also times after college that I tried to compartmentalize my life. Living to fulfill my sinful desires during the week and then going to church on Sunday mornings, Bible study on Wednesday nights or singing in the choir. Matthew 6: 24 tells us that we can't serve two masters (KJV). This verse is talking about God and money, but it wouldn't take too much of a stretch of the imagination for it to fit this situation as well. You see the more we submit to doing what feels good to our body, the more we will want to do it. Then getting up to go to church on Sunday morning is no longer something you have the privilege of doing, but instead just a chore you have to do. Just something you do because you feel it's what's supposed to be done. Eventually you start to resent God and come up with excuses to get out of it altogether. When you are juggling a double life it's only a matter of time until one of the balls falls. And you don't usually drop the one you enjoy the most.

Up until this point I have focused a lot on the role of water in the development and growth process of a tree. But while doing my research I learned that in order for a tree or vine branch to bear fruit, all the necessary conditions must be met. One adverse condition can either decrease fruit production or prevent it altogether. This is why God's role as the vineyard keeper is so important. He knows what we need to grow into who he created us to be. This is why it's important to know that when winter comes it's not the time to give up. Instead, it is the time to dig your roots in and brace yourself for what's to come. Some fruit trees like Peach and plum must have a specific number of hours of cold in winter in order for their flower buds to open in spring. If they don't get the cold they need, the tree will not produce fruit. We serve a God who is able to do what is described in Genesis 50:20, take what is intended to harm us and make it turn out for our good. God does some of his best work during the winter. Also let's not forget after winter comes spring, the season of growth.

God is able to provide the perfect conditions under which we will obtain optimum growth. One of those conditions is son-light. When there is not enough sunlight fruit production can be delayed and the amount greatly reduced. God sent his son Jesus to be the light of the world. If we stay connected to him, we will bear much fruit. Jesus is the best example of how to live and love. Accepting him is the beginning of our relationship with God and apart from him we can do nothing. Acknowledging his existence is not enough, we must follow him and strive to be like him.

In the forest there are four positions that individual trees can have in the canopy. Dominant trees, Co dominant trees, intermediate trees, and overtopped trees. Dominant trees are the tallest trees in the canopy. They receive light from above as well as from the side. They are the trees that stick up in the horizon towering over the other trees around them. They are usually also the thickest trees. Jesus is the dominant tree. He is the perfect example of taking full advantage of the growth conditions provided by God. He knew what God had called him to do and despite what it cost him; his response was "not what I will but what you will" Mark 14: 36

Codominant trees make up your tree line. They are shorter than the dominant trees. There are usually many trees at this level. These trees make up the average height of the trees in the forest. They get direct sunlight from above and may even receive a little direct sunlight from the sides. The best, we as Christians can hope for in this life is to be a codominant tree. As codominant trees we strive to take full advantage of growth conditions like the dominant tree, but our human frailty and our fleshly desires make that impossible. However, God is fully aware of our abilities and our limitations, he has the perfect plans to prosper us and to give us hope and a future as it says in Jeremiah 29: 11. So as codominant trees as long as we stay connected to our source and acknowledge and submit to his will for our lives we will flourish.

Intermediate trees get some direct light from above but none from the side. They will not be as thick as the dominant or codominant trees nor as tall. Intermediate trees represent believers that have either not yet connected to the source or who were connected and instead chose to disconnect from the source. The belief in Jesus as our savior is there, so we receive some of his light. However, when the winter months of life come, they affect us so harshly that we are unable to thrive and bear fruit. And instead of times of struggle growing our faith as it should, it keeps us stagnant unable to grow into all that God desires for us. This can also be the case with those of us who value our leaves more than bearing fruit and those of us living double lives.

The overtopped trees get no direct sunlight. They actually seek indirect light. Can you imagine wanting to live in the shadows. Shadow is equal to darkness. This is why they are shorter, have much less leaves. They could grow bigger and thrive in full son, but they have adapted to live in full shade. For this reason, they grow smaller and slower. Overtopped trees represent unbelievers. They have adapted to following the ways of this world. They cannot live up to their full potential because they have not acknowledged their need for direct access to the son, which is step one. Because of their inability to see the need for the son, they prefer to exist in the shade. For some it may be that, because they have always been in the shade, they don't realize that full son-light and all its benefits are available to them. Unfortunately for others they feel that because they have learned to flourish in the shade, the light that is offered from the son is not worth the sacrifice of living in God's will.

The most amazing thing about serving our God is that disconnection is not permanent. No matter what level we may find ourselves in, whether it's intermediate or overtopped, with God there is always an opportunity for growth. Once we acknowledge our need for God, he is willing and ready for us to reconnect.

Questions

1. Read 1Timothy 2: 4-6 what is the truth God wants us to come to the knowledge of?

2. Read revelation 22: 17 what stood out to you in this verse?

3. Has there ever been a time in your life that you feel you traded your intimacy with God for a piece of fruit? What was the fruit?

4. Are you bearing fruit or just producing leaves?

5. Has there ever been a time in life when you lived a double life? What made you realize that it was happening?

6. Being Honest with yourself, what position do you feel you hold in the canopy? Are you satisfied with that position? If not, is it worth it to you to do what it takes to grow?

7. Do you find it harder to stay connected during times of abundance or struggle? Why?

Chapter Notes

CHAPTER FIVE

THE 5 R'S OF RECONNECTION

Now that we see we can disconnect from the source, how can we remedy that situation? I think the first thing to acknowledge is that because we were born into sin, being connected to God as our source is not our default setting. On the contrary it is a choice we must continually make. We must acknowledge our need for him and then accept him. All of which goes against our human nature. But by the grace of God, when we realize that apart from him, we can do nothing and come to receive him as our Lord and savior. Then God (the gardener) gets to work. That's when we gain access to the living water. That water that becomes a spring welling up to eternal life. That water which quenches our thirst. To me this thirst can mean different things. It can be a longing for companionship or even a realization that there is something missing in our lives. Thirst, in and of itself reveals a need. I believe that once we allow God to meet that need in our life, we will not have to long for anything else.

GRAFTING

I like to think of the process that happens after we accept Jesus as grafting. Grafting is placing a part of one plant into or onto a branch, stem, or root of another. When this is done it forms a union between the two and they will continue to grow together. The word union used in this way reminds me of Ephesians 5: 22-33 when Paul uses the analogy of the union of marriage in description of the relationship between Christ and the church. When we take that first step and are united with Jesus, we have been grafted to the vine. Grafting is done for many reasons; to repair injured trees, help strengthen resistance to climate, disease, and conditions, and to produce certain types of fruit. These examples of a trees' need to be grafted also demonstrate the reasons for our need to be grafted as well. When we are hurting and in despair and the vine keeper grafts us to the vine, we receive nourishment that heals us. Once we are connected to the vine, we become stronger. We are no longer at the mercy of our circumstances. The situations we find ourselves in don't dictate our peace because we receive peace from the vine. We are better equipped to resist the temptation of sin because the vine provides our needs. We are not blown away by the winds of trouble because we are anchored to the vine. Once the grafting process is complete, we get the opportunity to bear fruit. Paul uses the analogy of us being grafted in Romans 11: 16-20, he says that we were wild olive shoots that were grafted in. He takes the time to inform us that it's not us supporting the root but instead the root that is supporting us. We were grafted in because of our faith. What a blessing it is that just by accepting Jesus Christ as our savior, believing, and having faith in him, we are able to become a part of his body. There are not a lot of hoops to jump through nor hurdles to cross. Just faith, we receive the greatest gift available to man, eternal life, just by having faith.

RE-GRAFTING

All that covers us being grafted in as a new follower of Christ. But what happens when we realize that we have been disconnected and then want to reconnect? Well Paul gives us hope in that scenario as well. In Romans 11: 23-24 it gives us hope that God has the ability to re-graft us in again when we come back to him. This isn't just a God job though; we must play our part in the process as well. We have done step one, realizing that we are no longer connected to the source. The next thing we must do, which often happens simultaneously with the first, is make the choice to reconnect. Sometimes that choice can be easy to make and sometimes it's hard. As I said in an earlier chapter my disconnection came during a time of abundance. There was no health scare, financial hardship, or troubled relationship that could send me to God on my knees praying. My disconnection was not uncomfortable... At first.

However, when I was at a point in my life when I thought we were on the doorsteps of foreclosure. My relationship with God was my constant. It was the one part of my life that was on a solid foundation. I talked to him all day every day for comfort, peace, and yes help, out of that situation. For some reason it took a while to get to the help part. But I thank him for his comfort and peace on this journey. You see I have become a pro at running to the Father when life is tough. But, when life is flowing like a river and I now have to turn and take the step towards God, toward reconnection. For some reason it's hard. The perceived freedom I thought I had renders making the right daily choices even more difficult. I did what my sinful nature wanted and justified it. Those desires and justifications are different for everyone. Maybe we shop with reckless abandoned. Amazon boxes showing up to our houses every day. It's a hard habit to break. To climb our way out of that materialistic pit. We may find ourselves in this world of Lil Flip where we see it, want it, buy it, flaunt it. We often show off what we have so people will be impressed by our stuff. But maybe materialism is not an issue for you. Maybe a glass of wine every now and then with dinner has somehow become a bottle of wine every night before bed.

Or perhaps scrolling a few minutes before bed turned into constantly checking your favorite social media platforms every few minutes and losing hours of sleep despite the guy popping up reminding you to take a break. Just because we have chosen to reconnect doesn't mean that we no longer see it and want it. It doesn't take the desire for wine away, and when we log into that favorite app our brain doesn't stop secreting that happy hormone dopamine. No all the above still happens, but we have to choose this day and every day whom we will serve, and if the goal is to be connected to God as our source that choice must be the Lord.

REBUILDING

Now that we have made the choice, we are on to Step 3. Rebuilding our relationship. This takes intentionality and perseverance on our part. We must be willing to do the work.

The drinking, overspending, social media addiction, and anything else we might struggle with are symptoms. I have been guilty of putting an app timer on my phone, so I won't get carried away and spend too much time on social media. I have even deleted apps I felt were distracting me from what was important and taking up too much of my time. But those actions, even though they were helpful for a little while, only managed the symptoms. They did not cure my disease. As I said before, sinfulness is a disease and the only treatment is a relationship with God, our father.

I had high blood pressure because I tend to focus my stress internally and I'm a fan of anything with bacon or fried, and in some cases with bacon AND fried. The doctor put me on medication to lower my blood pressure. The medication treated my symptoms, meaning it did lower my blood pressure, but the medication didn't treat the disease. It did not fix the problem. I had to change my diet, deal with my stressors, and commit to being more active and healthier overall. Once I did that, I was now treating the disease. Each time after that, when I went to the doctor for a checkup, she would decrease my dosage until finally she took me off the medication altogether. There was nothing wrong with me taking blood pressure medication because it did what it was supposed to do. However, if I had not treated my disease, I would be on those pills for the rest of my life. See, I'm not saying don't take steps to treat the symptoms. Stop drinking, put timers and limits on your phone, delete apps, and stay away from your triggers. But if you don't forge a real lasting relationship with God, you will have to do these things for the rest of your life. Then one day you may find that just managing the symptoms, and never treating the disease has allowed it to progress to the point where what you're doing no longer works. The best thing we can do is seek healing from the father, because while we are managing our symptoms, He is healing our heart. And one day we'll look up and find that we no longer have to put timers, limits and delete people and apps because through our relationship with Him, our disease is being forced into remission.

I don't care who you talk to if you ask a married couple what they think are the top three keys to making a relationship work. Communication is going to be somewhere in that top three. The same can be said for our relationship with God. We must talk to him through prayer. We cannot just go through the motions we must be honest and vulnerable. Truly desire to share with him and trust him to listen. 1 Thessalonians 5: 17 tells us to pray continually. Ephesians 6: 18 tells us to pray on all occasions with all kinds of prayers and requests. Matthew 26: 41 tells us to watch and pray so we won't fall into temptation. Luke 18: 1 tells us that we should always pray and not give up. He even taught us how to pray in Luke 11. Those are just a few scriptures that highlight the importance of prayer. God desires to hear from us, He's our father. We don't have to wax poetically to come to him in prayer. All we have to do is honestly and humbly bring our cares to him good or bad, big or small.

How many of us have been in a one-sided conversation with someone. They just talk and talk, and you are unable to get a word in edgewise? Was that a fulfilling and productive conversation? I am guessing your answer to that question is no. Therefore, we shouldn't want that type of communication with God. If all we do is pray, when do we give God a chance to speak to us. That's not communication that's a lecture and God doesn't need a lecture from us. Truth be told he already knows what's going on. Prayer is for the benefit of our relationship with him, not to inform him of our circumstances.

Now I have heard people say they can audibly hear the voice of God. Other people say he speaks to them through dreams. Now none of this may be true for you. But I know for sure one way that he communicates to us all. Through his holy word. No matter where we are in our Christian walk, whether we have read the Bible from cover to cover many times. Or we are just opening it up for the first time, God can speak to us through scripture. I can't tell you how many times God has spoken to my circumstances through his word. Sometimes to encourage, sometimes to teach, sometimes to correct, but always out of love.

REFLECT

Now that the lines of communication are open, it's time for step four. To reflect. It's time to reflect on all the ways God has been there for us and made ways for us throughout our lives. It's time to look back at his footprints in the sand. The reason this is important is because it gives us a foundation to move from trust in God to confidence in God. It gives us the evidence we need to conclusively say He is my fortress; He is my foundation; He is my source.

It is inevitable that whenever my family gets together, we will somehow end up reminiscing on the good old days. We tell stories and laugh. It's interesting how we can even find joy in looking back at the hard times. Sharing this reminds us of our connections and how we have always been there with and for each other. It reminds us of our roots. Our bond is strengthened through our shared experiences. My kids get to know me a little better by hearing about the good, the bad, and yes even the embarrassing parts of my life growing up. It also helps them learn about family members that may have already passed on.

It's the same when we reflect on the goodness of God. It reminds us of our connection to him, how he has always been there for us. It reminds us that he has been our source and strengthens our bond with him. When our children hear about our experiences with him it gives them an idea of who he has been to us and an example of who he can be to them. It helps start the foundation of their relationship with God.

However, during this time of reflection, we can't just think about all that God has done for us. It is important that we also investigate how and why the connection was severed in the first place. For me life was good. I can explain it like going into the ocean when you cannot swim. I walked in and the water was up to my ankles. It felt good so I went in a little farther to my knees and I could feel the sand between my toes. I knew I would be OK if I went a little deeper in letting the water come up to my waist. At that depth the water would sway me from side to side, but my feet were still firmly planted beneath me, so I felt I was fine. It was even a little exhilarating and fun, so I kept going. Once it got up to my shoulders though, I noticed that when the water would come in, it would be uncomfortably close to my mouth and the sand beneath my feet would start to shift. The movement of the water controlled me more than I could control myself, and when I turned to look back to the shore it seemed so far away. The time for me to turn back wasn't when the water was at my shoulders, nor my waist, not even at my knees. The time for me to turn back was at my ankles when I was choosing to walk into a situation that was beyond my ability to control. I never planned to go in that deep but the deeper I went with no adverse reaction the more trust I had in my ability to handle it. No, I didn't jump feet first into the deep end. I relied more on what felt good than on my God who IS good. When this happens it's like we get further and further from God with each step we take. With each choice we make. With each item we buy. With each glass we drink. And with each swipe and scroll. It is easy to look at it like we are just buying the things that we want not realizing we may not be being good stewards of what God has given us. It's easy to say well God turned water into wine so why can't I drink a couple of glasses. Not understanding that one of the fruit of the spirit is self-control and when we consume too much alcohol it takes away our ability to demonstrate that fruit of the spirit. It's easy to scroll without realizing that it is giving us FOMO. Making us envious and jealous of what we see and ungrateful for what we have. We must look back to find the point in time in which we chose what we wanted to do instead of what God would have us to do. Now I don't think any of these things are sinful in and of themselves. But even something innocent can take a wrong turn if we are using it to be disobedient to God.

Now we have to look at the why. There was something that the enemy dangled in front of our face that we chose not to resist. Why? Was it arrogance thinking that we know what's best and how best to deal with things. Maybe it was the snowball effect where it started out as something innocent but the more we partook of it the less we controlled it and the more it controlled us. Or maybe we allowed our sinful nature to take over, forcing our self-control into the back seat. Regardless of what we may find as we reflect, we have to search for the reason so we can learn from it and not repeat it.

REPENTANCE

The next step is repentance. Now that we have reflected on how and why, it's time to sincerely express our remorse about walking away. When we repent, we turn from the ways of our sinful nature and turn to the way of our God. This is turning twice, mathematically speaking it is a 180-degree turn. Which is a complete change in direction. To me this means that once we complete steps one through four, we make a complete change in direction for our life. We don't go through all the previous steps to just stay the same, do the same, be the same. If we do that then we are missing the point. Yes, we have a gracious and forgiving God but Romans 6: 1-4 tells us that we can't continue on in our sin just because God is gracious. Once we accepted Christ we died to our sins and were raised with Christ in a newness of life. Like I said before, repenting is a complete change in the direction you were going. When we would normally follow our own whims and do whatever tickles our fancy, now we take God into consideration. You see when we have a relationship with God, he allows us to be convicted when we have done something that we know would not be pleasing in his sight.

On one of my many grocery shopping trips, I had gone through the checkout line, and I was back in my car on my way home. As I drove, I did the math in my head because I felt like I should have paid more for what I had gotten that day. The more I thought of it, the more it just didn't quite add up. Once I finally got home, I thought I had figured out what the problem was and now I just needed to confirm it. I searched through the bags and found my receipt. When I looked at my receipt my thoughts were confirmed. The lady that checked me out had only charged me for one package of cupcakes. I honestly didn't want to go back to the store and truth be told I really only had enough cash to cover the amount that she had charged me. Plus, I needed to take those cupcakes to my daughter's school the next morning so her class could celebrate her birthday. Not to mention, who would even know. I had gotten out of the store and all the way home before I had figured out what happened. It wasn't like I had done it on purpose. I didn't go into the store with the intent to take a package of cupcakes without paying. I didn't even try to hide them or anything. The cashier had both packages but only scanned one. It was not my fault. But God convicted me and reminded me that no matter what an inconvenience it was, it was my responsibility as a child of the King to act accordingly and to go back and pay for that package of cupcakes. So, I did. Not for acknowledgment or accolades. But because it was what God would have me do.

You see God convicts us. Shows us when and how we are wrong so that we can make it right or not make the same mistake twice. The enemy, however, loves to condemn us. He wants us to feel guilty and hold on to that guilt, believing that God could not forgive us because what we've done was so bad. The reason for this condemnation is to cause separation between us and God. All he has to do is get us to believe the lie that God doesn't love us or can't love us because of something we have done or because we are unlovable. But the sheer fact that we exist makes us loved by God. Condemnation is all about punishment while conviction is all about acknowledging that what you have done is wrong. You can be convicted of a crime and be pardoned. That is in essence what Jesus did for us. We were convicted of our sins, but Jesus paid the price. We have been pardoned and forgiven.

RECEIVE

Now that we have repented, we must choose to receive God's forgiveness. It seems like such an easy step. But a lot of times we can get stuck on Step 5 and hold on to guilt over what we have done. One of the amazing things about our God is that when he forgives, he forgives completely. Psalms 103: 12-13 tells us that he removes our transgressions from us as far as the east is from the West. Because he has compassion for us like a father has compassion for his children. Doubling back to the idea of a pardon. When a defendant is offered a pardon he or she can accept or deny it. That means that forgiveness can be offered but the defendant may not accept it. Now you may be thinking who in their right mind would reject a pardon, an opportunity to be relieved of the consequences resulting from their wrongdoing. Well, that is what we do when we don't freely receive the forgiveness given to us by God. We allow the guilt and shame of what we did (that which God has already forgiven us from) to fester and get to be so big in our eyes that it becomes the lens with which we see ourselves through. Instead of it being something we did, it becomes who we are. An out of wedlock mother, an alcoholic, a drug addict, etcetera. But God sees you as he created you. As a child of the one true king. So, we must see ourselves how he sees us and receive his mercy, receive his grace, receive his love, and receive his forgiveness. There is no need to continue to sit in the space you were in when God has called you out of that space and into more. The more that he has planned for you, the more he created you for. There he is standing at the door knocking just waiting for you to open the door so he can come in. God is not going to force himself on you. You must make the choice to receive what he is offering. You must make the choice to reconnect to the source.

Questions

1. Have you ever found yourself justifying actions that you know don't line up with God's will for you? Elaborate.

2. Has there ever been a time in your life that you felt you were treating the symptoms instead of the disease?

3. When you go to God in prayer, do you feel you allow yourself to be completely vulnerable? If not, what is holding you back?

4. Take a moment to reminisce on a time when God came through for you, made a way for you, provided for, or healed you, etc.

5. Think about a time, if any, that you were disconnected from God. Can you pinpoint the choice that was the first step to that disconnection?

6. Has there ever been a time when something good or innocent turned into something the devil used to try to lure you away from God? If yes, explain.

7. Have you ever found it hard to accept the forgiveness God is offering? If yes, why?

Chapter Notes

CHAPTER SIX

THE GOOD LIFE

Welcome to the good life! Now I don't want you to think I call it the good life because nothing bad will ever happen to you. Unfortunately, that is what many of us think. When we make the choice to surrender our lives over to God and accept him as our Lord and savior, we think we should be on easy street. We feel the trials and tribulations of life are behind us. But no that is not the case. Then why do I call it the good life? Because it is a life connected to the one true source. I call it the good life because no matter what we go through we always know that our heavenly father will be there with us. He is not even a call away because he already knows when we will need him, and he is there. He just waits on us to acknowledge that need and reach out to him.

Today my husband and I went to pick up some wings we ordered for lunch. He went in to get the food while I waited in the car. As I sat there, I looked out of the car window admiring the vastness and the beauty of the trees in the distance. I noticed how tall they were and the splendor they possessed. I also noticed the multitude of different shades of green and shapes of leaves. I observed how the contrast of the green of the leaves, marred next to the blue of the sky, complemented each other, and formed the magnificence of the landscape before me.

It is spring now, so all the trees have vibrant green leaves. The magnolias have even started to open their buds sending their fragrance through the air. There is so much beauty in this season. So much so that it makes us almost forget about winter. It is the same way in our lives. Sometimes the good times can be so good that the tribulations fade into the background. But we can't allow that to happen because everything; Good bad and in between, everything that happens in our lives has a purpose. James, Jesus's brother tells us in James 1: 2-3 that even the winter months serve a purpose. He tells us that trials test our faith and produce perseverance. If you go through a trial and you don't draw closer to God, or your faith is not increased it is a waste of a good trial.

I have touched on the Israelites and their journey to the promised land before but one thing I wrote about in one of my journals back in June 2016 was the timing of God. If he wanted, God could have parted the Red Sea when the Israelites were still a long way off. Before the Egyptian army was even in pursuit. However, faith is a muscle that needs to be exercised and if the Israelites would have come to the obstacle with it already being remedied then there would be no need for them to have faith. However, in allowing them to get to the Red Sea and have it raging in front of them, plus pharaoh and his army horseshoeing them in. It forced them to dig deep and find some hope and faith. This also gives them an experience of God making a way so they will have confidence in him when they get to another "Red Sea". Working on that faith muscle then, and all the other times he came through for them during those 40 years, made their faith strong. Some of that 40-year-old Red Sea faith gave Joshua the confidence he needed to know that God would deliver the city of Jericho into their hands. They could pull from their Red Sea workout and have hope, faith, and confidence that following God's directions about marching around a walled city would cause the wall to crumble down. That God would deliver it into their hands. Sometimes God puts us in a situation where the problem gets fixed in the ninth hour because he wants us to trust that he will take care of us. Then we will approach the next obstacle with a Philippians 4: 6 mindset. Being anxious about nothing but by prayer and petition with thanksgiving, presenting our request to him.

As I told you before, our family went through a period of financial struggle. We didn't have the ability to pay our mortgage for a few months. My husband reached out to our mortgage company to let them know we still didn't have the money and were not going to be able to make the next month's payment either. The gentleman on the other line informed my husband about a program that would give us relief and we wouldn't have to make any payments for three months. We applied for the program and were approved for it the same day. That was a complete blessing. Because of all the other times in our lives that he had made a way I was confident that my God would fix our situation. He did not fix it the way I thought he would, but he did fix it and I thank him for that. A life connected to the source doesn't mean your journey will be easy, but it does mean you won't have to journey alone.

I spent this time at the beginning of this chapter on this concept because I feel it is very important to know. Some of us get disconnected because we have trials and tribulations in our lives, and we feel that we shouldn't have to face these problems because we have a relationship with God. So, when obstacles come, we run, we disconnect because what's the point of being connected if I still have issues and complications in my life. One thing I want you to know is that having a perfect life in an imperfect world is impossible. If that is what you're looking for I can tell you right now, it's not going to happen. But I can share with you what a life connected to the source can look like, it's not perfect but there can be beauty in imperfection.

Trees are made up of many different parts that all serve a purpose. When all the parts are working together the tree flourishes. Let's start from the bottom up.

ROOTS

The roots' main functions are to anchor the tree, absorb water and nutrients from the soil, send them to the trunk for distribution, and store carbohydrates for energy during winter. When you plant a seed the first part that grows is the root. The primary focus of that seed is to have a firm foundation to grow from. Our souls need to be anchored in the Lord. Our acceptance of him as our savior is the firm foundation from which we grow as Christians. Paul tells us in 1 Corinthians 3: 11 that no one can lay any foundation other than the one already laid, which is Jesus Christ. As I said before there are numerous scriptures in the Bible that refer to God as water. Through our roots we absorb God in, we receive all that we need to survive and be maintained from him. Once we absorb him in, we allow him access to every part of our being. All of who we are and all of what we have. Carbohydrates represent our faith. Our faith is stored in our foundation, Jesus. When tough times come (winter) we draw on our faith to sustain us.

TRUNK

A tree's trunk is made-up of many different layers. The older the tree is, the wider its trunk becomes. That is why it is said you can tell how old a tree was by counting its rings. The rings not only tell how old the tree is, but they can also give us insight into the conditions that the tree has encountered throughout its life. Scientists can tell by studying the rings whether it was a rainy season or a dry season. They can even tell if a tree had survived a forest fire in past years. In the years that are warm with an increase of rain the rings are wider. However, in years when it is cold and dry the rings are thinner. Regardless of the conditions though, every year the tree grows. Every day with our Lord and Savior is an opportunity to grow in relationship with him. Every situation we allow him to bring us through strengthens us and gives us the support we need to be stronger for the next obstacle we face. Our rings are our memories. They help us to look back and see the times when God has brought us through the fire. As well as the times when the winter months were so dry that we clung to him for support and sustainability. But they also remind us of the good times. When he bathed us in abundance and blessings. Through each season with our Lord and Savior, our trunk becomes wider, and we become stronger.

One of the main functions of a tree's trunk is support. Our old house had an oak tree in the front yard. It was as tall as our house. And the trunk was so wide that I don't think my son's hands would touch it if he wrapped his arms around it. However, the oak tree at our current home was planted during construction. It's about 8 foot tall and if I grabbed it by the trunk with both my hands my fingers would touch. When we first moved in, there were these three steel rods surrounding the tree staked into the ground to stabilize it until the roots grew into the soil. I looked into how long I should keep those stuck in place and found I should remove the steak after 6 to 12 months depending on the tree type. I read that allowing those stakes to remain in place for too long can hinder the strength of the trunk. According to a study done in Illinois, trees that remained staked too long were tall, but weaker due to a smaller trunk diameter. They found that trees need to sway freely in the wind so that their trunks will grow stronger. As a Christian I have found that I myself also come out of the storm and winds of my life stronger, as well as with an increased dependency on God. If I allow the stake of religion to control me; Doing what others expect me to do, acting how others expect me to act. Checking all the right religious boxes but leaving all the relational ones blank. Really just going through the motions of what is supposed to be done, trying to earn my way. I.e., Going to church because of the good music or because it's what I did every Sunday growing up, may get me in the door but only a real intimate relationship with the savior will sustain me. Without it I will miss out on an opportunity to become strong and sturdy through a relationship with a father who will be there with me as I face the winds of life. Ensuring that though I may sway I will be stronger because of it.

BRANCHES

The next part I want to touch on are the branches. Branches give structural support to the leaves, fruit and/or flowers produced by the tree. They also channel water from the trunk to the leaves and food from the leaves to the rest of the tree. Branches are attracted to the sun and try to grow towards it to give the leaves as much light as possible. When we live a life connected to the source our branches are the fruit of the spirit as found in Galatians 5: 22. As I touched on in Chapter 1 these are the parts of our life that reflect Jesus, our source of derivation. Our branches reflect the Son. There are two things I find remarkably interesting about the fruit of the spirit. The first is that though there are nine traits, it is called the fruit of the spirit not the fruits of the spirit. This leads me to believe that my Lord possesses all these simultaneously and because I am derived from him so will I. That means I can't strive to have joy but ignore kindness. Likewise, I can't practice patience but not self-control and so on. The other interesting thing is looking back at Matthew 7: 20 which I will paraphrase, "you can know a tree by the fruit it bears" gives me the understanding that we will be known as a follower of Christ not because of the just God T-shirts or Jesus tattoos but instead by our love, joy, peace, patience, kindness, goodness, faithfulness, gentleness, and self-control. The greatest hope about this is that the fruit of the spirit is a byproduct of living a life connected to the source. I like the way the new living translation proceeds the list. It says "but the Holy Spirit produces this kind of fruit in our lives..." you notice it didn't say if we love God, we will be patient, kind, etc. Instead, to me at least, I understand it as saying that being connected to the source will give us the ability to be faithful, gentle, self-controlled, etc. So, I don't have to figure out how to love someone who is not being loving towards me. Nor do I have to figure out how to have peace in the midst of my storms. All I have to do is lean and depend on God and choose to respond to the situations of life with the abilities he has already given me. By no means am I saying as soon as you start your relationship with God you will magically be able to respond to every situation with the requisite fruit of the Spirit. Not at all.

My youngest daughter doesn't like to have anyone do anything medical to her. Whether that's giving shots or cleaning up a Boo Boo. So, one day I needed to put something in her nose, and she was not having it. She ran away and when I told her to come back, she started to cry. It was honestly nothing that would even hurt her, but she was afraid it would hurt. The more I tried to coax her the more enraged she became and the more she bawled. My response to her was not one of self-control and gentleness but instead frustration and anger. I was immediately convicted because of my reaction, but we both needed to calm down. So, I suggested we each retreat to our separate areas for a minute or maybe an hour. After a little time had passed, I called her back in and apologized for my behavior. Then I figured out a way to get done what needed to be done with patience and understanding of who she is and respect for her fears. I had the ability to be patient and gentle during our first attempt, but I didn't choose to respond with that ability. Instead, I chose to be reactionary. The best thing about this story is that I remember a time when I would not have called a ceasefire and ordered a retreat to our separate corners to calm down. I definitely would not have apologized. So, I see the work he's doing in me. I see the growth. Also, the closer I get to him I see that I respond to more of life's situations with the ability he has produced in me.

Choosing to live out the fruit in our everyday lives goes against our human nature. But I will say it's like learning to tie a shoe or ride a bike, it takes practice.

LEAVES

If you will remember from Chapter 2 that the leaves represent the external part of us. Our leaves are what we show to the world. They are our persona, personality, lifestyle, and character. The leaves are the most visible part of the tree. It is definitely what we notice first. We judge a tree by its leaves. If a tree has a lot of leaves, we assume it's a healthy and vibrant tree. If a tree doesn't produce leaves in season, we deem it to be dead. It is the same with us. If our lifestyle is thriving and we post pictures on social media with #blessed underneath. People assume we have it all together and we are #goals. But if our personality and/or persona is lacking. People write us off, assuming that we are unproductive and dead. Just like the presence or appearance of leaves on a tree does not necessarily tell you all you need to know about a tree. Our leaves don't necessarily always tell you all you need to know about us.

Early on in my Christian walk when things would get tough, and trials would come I would shed my leaves. People who knew me knew that I was going through something because my continence would be down. I may not be as talkative as I would normally be, and I wouldn't do the things I would normally do. My leaves would shed for the same reason a tree's leaves would shed, for preservation. It would take all I had to keep the faith and continue to hope during those times. I didn't have any extra "water" to excrete through my leaves because I was using it all to sustain me. So, I had to let them fall.

Now however, I find that with each tribulation I go through the more leaves I maintain. I can be happy for someone who is going through a season of abundance in an area that I am experiencing lack. I can be a blessing to someone when I need one myself. The reason for this change is because I am starting to realize what God said long ago in Deuteronomy 31: 8, that the Lord will never leave me nor forsake me. Then in Philippians 4:19 that he will supply all my needs. And finally in Romans 8: 38-39 which lets me know that nothing can separate me from his love. So, you see, my leaves are being maintained because I am connected to, and I have confidence in, my source. Knowing the battle has already been won on your behalf makes retaining leaves during the battle more probable.

Leaves serve a purpose; they are not there just to make the trees look nice. The leaves job is to make food. They use energy from the sunlight, carbon dioxide and water to make the food for the tree. This process is called photosynthesis which means to make something <u>new</u> using <u>light</u>. Jesus tells us in John 8: 12 that he is the light for the world. When we follow Him, we will no longer walk in darkness but instead we will have a life that is made new using the one true light. God nourishes us with this "new" life given to us by his son and our Lord and Savior. When we accept this new life, our leaves start to change. We look up one day and realize that through this journey with our Lord he has done what it said he would do in psalms 37: 4 give us the desires of our heart. Not meaning that he will actually give me whatever my heart desires. But it means he will instead place the desires he wants me to have, in my heart. The longer we stay connected to the source we will find that our desires start to mirror his desires. When this happens our personality, the things we say and do change. Our persona, how people see us, changes. Our lifestyle, where we go and how we spend our time and money changes. As well as our character, what we value and think changes. It is through these changes in our leaves that we are positioned to bear fruit.

FRUIT

Bearing fruit is the duty Jesus gave us after his resurrection. He instructed us in Matthews 28: 19-20 to make disciples of all nations teaching them to obey what he commanded of us. That's what bearing fruit is, it's leading others to Christ. It is showing up in their lives being the hands and feet of God and then earning a right to share the story of what God has done for us in hopes that God will use what we share to open someone up and soften their hearts, so they would choose him and his way. Incredibly trees have DNA just like humans, and that DNA instructs them how to produce fruit. They are programmed to produce fruit. If you took anatomy and Physiology in high school, you will know that our DNA comes from our parents. So spiritually our DNA comes from our heavenly father. When we accept him and connect to him as our source, bearing fruit is a part of our spiritual DNA. It is a trait we inherit from our father.

In our everyday lives we enjoy the taste of and benefits from the nourishment of fruit. However, the real purpose of the part of the fruit we consume is to protect and spread the seed. We focus on the flesh of fruit because it is visible and edible. We enjoy it because it looks and tastes good. When we eat an apple or a plum, we enjoy the sweet fleshy part of the fruit while treating the seeds as an inconvenience to be disposed of. However, to a tree the seed is the most important part. The flesh is only created around the seed to protect it and attract animals to it so that the seed will someday become a tree of its own. You see the seed; is the way the fruit tree reproduces. So, when fruit falls to the ground and gets eaten by an animal the seed which is what's left is often taken to a different location and fertilized by the animal. Eventually that seed starts to sprout and grow. If we do what we should our fruit will mature, falloff, be fertilized, and grow into its own tree. That is how we make disciples. Matthew 12: 33 tells us that a tree is known by its fruit. When we live a life connected to the source we share about the goodness of God (the gardener and water) so that others can come to know him and accept him as their Lord and Savior. Then they mature enough to sprout, digging into the firm foundation of Jesus Christ. Ultimately growing in relationship with our God. Becoming their own tree, being maintained by the vine keeper, sustained by the water, and eventually producing their own fruit.

PRUNING

Trees are pruned to help strengthen them and limit the likelihood of damage during harsh weather. They are also pruned to cut away parts that may have disease or decay so that it won't spread to the healthy parts of the tree. Another reason to cut away part of the tree is to maximize sunlight exposure as well as air circulation. It also helps with fruit production because once the unproductive parts have been cut away, the resources (carbohydrates and water) that were being used to maintain the unproductive branches can now be reallocated to the fruit bearing branches.

There are many different benefits to pruning a tree. But have you ever thought about it from the tree's perspective? The tree is just minding its business doing its job as a tree when someone comes along and hacks off a part of it. I imagine that if a tree could feel, this process would be painful and confusing. I imagine that though the benefits of pruning are numerous, the action of pruning, to a tree, would probably seem like cruel and unusual punishment. The tree may feel like it could have healed that disease branch and brought that decaying twig back if it just allocated more resources to that part. It may feel that it's unfair to have someone come along and just take away a part of it without its permission. It's easy for me to imagine how a tree may feel because this is often how I feel when God prunes me.

There will be people places and things in our lives that God is going to have to cut away in order for us to grow. God sees into eternity past as well as eternity future so only he knows what's truly best for us. Because of this, he will take away the things, habits, and people, that will hinder our growth or spread disease and/or decay in our lives.

During my research into pruning, I found that if you prune a tree when you plant it and then one Year after that the need for future pruning will be moderate. Meaning you will only have to do maintenance pruning to keep the tree from getting too thick. This tells me that pruning is not just a one-time thing. It seems to me that as the tree grows and grows it will need some maintenance pruning to keep it on the right track. Isn't it ironic that the more you grow the more you will need to be pruned. Nona Jones called pruning a reward for fruitfulness.

With each new season of life as we grow and grow there are nouns, we grow out of. After God got us back on our feet from my husband being unemployed for two years and eight months, my relationship with him was deeper and closer than before. That is when I really started to hear from him. We had finally gotten our own place again and one day I was sitting down watching this show that I had always watched and enjoyed. But this time God told me not to watch it anymore. That show did not line up with his desires for me. I turned that show off and never watched it again. Did I enjoy watching the show, yes. Did I know other people that continued to watch the show, yes. But God didn't prune it from them, he pruned it from me. It is my job to trust that his reasons for it were to benefit me not to harm me. That's the thing, God's plans are not exactly the same for all of us. We don't grow at the same pace and our reasons for pruning are not the same. There may be things that God prunes from me that he allows to stay on you and vice versa. It's not my place or right to hold you to the same parameters God places on me. God deals with each of us in his own way and in his own time. My example was a TV show, but maybe for you it's a friendship or relationship. Maybe there is a job loss, or he may be directing you to quit your job without a backup plan. There may even be an unexpected and/or unwanted move. Whatever it may be, trust God through it. Trust that he knows what is best and that his reasons line up with his plans for you. When my husband lost that job and couldn't find another one, at first, I thought God was punishing us or had turned his back on us. The funny part is now that I have the benefit of looking back, I see that point and time in life was the first step to getting us on track. He used it to get us to where he wanted to take us. I see the opportunities that came out of it and the lessons learned from it. You see pruning can and most likely will be uncomfortable. But the growth you will experience and the fruit you will be able to bear because of it makes it worth it.

Questions

1. Have you ever felt that because you gave your life to God it shouldn't be this hard?

2. Have you ever been tempted to walk away from a relationship with God because of how hard. life is? Did you?

    a. Why or why not?

3. Have you ever felt constrained by the steaks of religion? Or have you ever used religion as a substitute for a relationship with God?

4. What is the one fruit of the spirit you feel you struggle with the most?

5. When trials come, are you more likely to shed your leaves or retain them?

6. Has there ever been a time in your life where God has placed on your heart to share your testimony with someone else? Did you do it?

7. Have you ever felt that God was pruning anyone or anything from your life?

Chapter Notes

CHAPTER 7

THE PERKS OF BEING CONNECTED

E very relationship has its perks. My husband is 6 '3 and in construction. One of the perks of being married to him is that I always have someone to reach the top shelf since I'm only 5'1. Another perk is that if I need anything put together or fixed, I can always get it done. I have a degree in education, so I'd like to think that not having to pay for preschool for all three of our children, because I home schooled them is a perk of being married to me. Plus, since I am arguably the best kitchen beautician we know, we rarely have to pay for trips to the hair salon. Which is great, because with me and my two girls all being natural, that cost adds up quickly.

Our relationship with God also has its perks. However, they far outweigh savings on hair salon visits and reaching the peanut butter off the top shelf in the pantry. The perks of being in relationship with our Heavenly Father enhances our life here on Earth and guarantees us an eternity with him in heaven. I could write a whole book about the perks of living a life connected to God as our source. But for now, I am just going to touch on two. The two I'm going to touch on are; the ability to communicate with the Holy Spirit and the Community of believers we become a part of. These are free benefits available to us. In these next two sections, I want to touch on these two perks that many of us often take for granted. It may be because we don't see them as perks. Or sometimes we can even view one or both of them as inconveniences instead. There are still others of us who do not take advantage of these perks at all because we are unaware of them.

THE COMMUNICATION WITH THE HOLY SPIRIT

As I stated previously, communication is not a one-way Street. He wants to be in conversation with us. In a conversation both parties speak and listen to each other. That is what God desires to have with us, a continuous conversation. In fact, he commands it. Through the apostle Paul, he tells us to pray continually in 1 Thessalonians 5: 17. No, I don't think he means for us to shut ourselves in our closets, lay prostrate, or sit with bowed head and closed eyes praying to him 24 hours a day, seven days a week. Though I do think that targeted devotional time spent in intimate prayer is required of us also. But in this verse, I believe he means thanking him for allowing you to see a new day when you open your eyes in the morning. Asking for patience when tackling the school morning routine with the kids, or gentleness so you won't get frustrated with the person that cuts you off on the way to work. Talk to him about the beauty of his creation as you see the blue sky and fluffy clouds before you. Stand in the gap for that coworker that is going through a tough time and lift them up to him as you pass their desk. Thank him for the food you have for lunch. Share your hopes for that promotion with him as you interact with your boss. Ask him for strength to persevere through the evening as you drive home tired. Thank him for his joy as you listen to the details of your kids or spouses' day. Implore him to watch over and keep you as you get into bed at night. At no time did you fall on your knees. But you acknowledged his presence, sovereignty, and your dependence upon him in your life. You prayed continually. And what happens when you pray? He responds.

The fact that we serve the one true God, the creator of the universe, and not only does he hear our prayers, but he wants us to pray to him. The ability for us to be in contact with him is such a privilege and a blessing. Talk about access!

I briefly touched on the Holy Spirit as the source of communication back in chapter one. As well as in Chapter 5 when I highlighted the importance of opening up the lines of communication when we reconnect to God as our source. But right now, I want to dive a little deeper into how having the Holy Spirit as our source of communication is a perk of being connected to, or in relationship with God. No matter where you are from or what language you speak, we all communicate with the same goal in mind. We all want to share information in a clear and concise way. No matter whether you are giving your friend directions to your house or talking a med student through their first Lap Chole. (I watch a lot of medical dramas.) We want to make sure our words are heard and understood. But truthfully, there is more to communicating than just talking. Yes, many of us communicate verbally, but we also communicate nonverbally as well as through written words or visual cues. And we must not forget one of the most important aspects of communication. Listening. And just like all the above is true in our communication with the people in our lives. It's also true for our communication with our Lord and Savior. Let's look at each of these facets of communication in relationship to the Holy Spirit.

VERBAL

As I have stated before, there are some who say they can audibly hear the voice of God directing and guiding them. I have experienced this at different times in my life. For me, it's not a deep Morgan Freeman voice telling me what to do. Instead, it's like a whisper in my mind. Like what is described in Isaiah 30:21. This has happened to me in the checkout line at the grocery store when the Whisperer instructed me to pay for the groceries of the person in front of me. It also happened at Church, when he directed me toward a complete stranger whom he wanted me to pull aside and pray with. There have been other instances as well. One of the most memorable times this happened is when we were house hunting. There was a house that I really liked by a certain builder. And I knew that was the one for me. However, when we went in to start the process to purchase the home, we found out the builder was on a selling freeze. The lady was helpful and showed us an inventory home they were going to build that was the same model as the house I liked. She told us she could save it for us, and we could put a contract on it. But we could not do so until after the foundation was poured. The land had not even been cleared yet, so that was going to be awhile. But we moved ahead, looking at design options for flooring and countertops. We would check back every week on the progress, and after two weeks the cost of the House went up. Because we were not under contract, we were told we couldn't lock in the price we were quoted originally. It was OK because it was still in our price range, albeit at the top, but still within what we could afford. The only problem is it went up again the next week. And again a few days after that. It had gone up so much that it was no longer in our budget. So, we made the tough decision to go look at other houses. We went on a Sunday to a model that my husband and I liked before. I never allowed myself to truly see it as our potential home because I was so enamored with the other house. If I'm being honest, I really wanted to go look at the model next door to the house my husband wanted to go to. But we went to the one he wanted to see first. When we walked in, we saw a printout with available inventory homes in the area, one caught our eye. But the salesperson had an appointment that was about to start, so he didn't have the time to talk with us about it. We waited for a few minutes and then decided to leave. As we were leaving, he came out and asked if we wanted to make an appointment with him so he could devote time to just speaking with us. We agreed and made plans to meet him the next day. As we left, I walked to the model next door so we could see what they had available. However, as I walked up to the house, I heard the whisper. It told me "Do not go in there. Turn around and go to the address of the house on the printout sheet you just saw". So that is what I did. Even though I was on the walkway a few steps from the front door, I turned around and we went to see the house from the sheet. It was just wood and house wrap, there was not even a roof. No really, you could see the sky while standing in the living room. But as soon as we walked in the makeshift front door, we knew it was our home, and that house is where I'm sitting as I write this.

You see, God didn't speak to me from the clouds like Mufasa did to Simba in The Lion King, but he did get his message across to me. If you have never experienced this, what I'm saying probably sounds unbelievable. But I promise it is true. I must admit that when I am seeking him in my everyday life and communicating with him, it happens more often. I honestly think that is because I am more open to him. Therefore, I notice his promptings more, which is good because it also means I am more likely to be obedient to what he is asking me to do. Because I was obedient, I could see that every step of the process of buying this House proved more and more that this was his plan all along. Therefore, making it better than anything we could have come up with on our own. Every obstacle and challenge we faced was met with a solution he had already formulated.

NON-VERBAL

The next way of communicating I would like to touch on is nonverbal. I can use the process of finding our new home as an example for this as well. When we stepped foot through the doorway of this "house" (I use the term loosely, remember it was only foundation and framing. No walls, no roofing.) a peace came over me. I felt at home among the wood, concrete and nails, and I could honestly say the more I walked around it felt right, it felt like home. This was not the first house we had looked at. I had walked into other houses in varying degrees of completion on many occasions. But none of them felt like home. I honestly believe that the peace of God had come over me as confirmation that this is where he wanted us to be. There is a purpose, a reason for us being here in this House, on this street with these neighbors. There were other times he has given me this peace as well. Like when my husband wanted to quit his job to start His business. Or when my dad was diagnosed with prostate cancer. In those situations, I could see Philippians 4: 6 demonstrated in my life. Because the peace that transcends all understanding did guard my heart and mind.

I have, however, also heard of the reverse happening to people. As it has happened to me this way as well. When there is an uneasy feeling about a place, a plan, or a decision. There have been times when I couldn't explain to my kids why the answer was no., I just knew that the answer needed to be no. Or we were getting everything together, but something just didn't feel right. Like it was not the right time or way to do this thing we were preparing to do. There's even been times when a decision has been made and my husband couldn't sleep at night. And it was constantly on his mind, and he knew that he needed to step back and pray before finalizing that decision. All the scenarios are the same. We never heard anything, but the feeling of peace either was or was not there. I think that is one of the ways God communicates with us nonverbally. The most important thing I can say about this nonverbal communication is that you must be open to God to receive it. Because it is nonverbal, if you are letting the noise of everyday life consume your mind and heart, you will be distracted and unable to see or feel what God is trying to express upon you. An example I can give of this from a parental perspective is when we went over to visit a friend and my middle child, my sensitive sweet one. Started distancing herself from the other kids. I was in a deep conversation with someone, talking about something I was very enthusiastic about (not really). But because I know her, I could tell from across the room that she needed my attention. I could just feel it. So, I got up from where I was. I went over to her and talked privately with her. Sure enough, something had happened, and she had had her fill and was ready to go home. Now, if I had been consumed with my conversation and what I had going on, I would have been too distracted to notice that she needed me. This is why it's important to spend time regularly in communication with God, because the more you spend time with him, the more you get to know him and his character. You learn what it's like to feel his presence. Just like I could tell what my daughter was communicating with me because I know her. We are able to tell that God is communicating with us when we know him.

WRITTEN

This leads me into the next way we receive communication from God. This is probably the most obvious way. The way most people would respond if asked the question; how does God communicate with us? It is written communication. Now the most recognizable written communication from God is the Bible. After all, 2 Timothy 3:16-17 tells us that all scripture is God breathed and is useful for teaching, rebuking, correcting, and training in righteousness, so that the servant of God may be thoroughly equipped for every good work. The Bible is a powerful weapon that we as Christian have in our arsenal. In Ephesians 6: 17, it tells us that the word of God is a sword. I don't know about you, but there is no way I would go into battle with a sword because not only have I never fought with one, but I have never even held one. Without proper training, a sword would be more detrimental than beneficial to me in a fight. Another example I can give to you is an open book test. I know from experience that being able to use my book on a test can go one of two ways. The first way and the most beneficial. Is if I have read the chapter, section, or book prior to the test. You see if I have previous experience with the information, I may not remember the exact answer, but I have an idea where to look to find it. Which makes it beneficial. The other way it could go is if I had not even cracked the spine of the book. If I had not read nor studied the book, I would not only not know the answer, but I would have no idea where to find it. Which would lead to me wasting time thumbing through pages hoping something pops out. That is how it is when we go through tests and trials in life. We have this book with this wealth of knowledge that can lead, guide, encourage, inspire, and uplift us. But because we have never even cracked the spine, when times get tough, we do not know where to go to look for the answer. When we read the word of God, we get an opportunity to learn about his character. We learned about his love for us in John 3: 16. We learn how he forgives us in Psalms 103: 12. We learn how he sees us in Isaiah 43: 4. But if you have never studied the word for yourself, you will believe the devil when he paints the picture of God as a tyrant that is only concerned with punishing us for our transgressions. Or when he tells you that you are worthless and unloved. But if you have read the Bible, you know nothing could be further from the truth.

VISUAL CUES

The next way we communicate is through visual cues. For all intent and purposes, we will equate this to signs. Signs can be a polarizing and controversial topic. But I genuinely believe that God does still give us signs. Even in this day and time. The sign that comes to mind right now for me, takes me back to buying our house. As I told you earlier, the salesperson asked if we would make an appointment so that he could devote his time and attention to just us. At the time he had another couple in his office that were also looking. So, we agreed. We made an appointment for the next day. As we drove home after making that appointment and going by to see the house that we fell in love with despite being only wood cement and nails. The date for the appointment just stuck out to me. When we got home. I took out my phone and opened my photos app and searched for the pictures we took the day we moved into the house we were living in at that time. To my surprise, when I clicked on the details, I saw that the date of the meeting with the salesperson was exactly seven years to the date that we had moved into that house. It is believed that seven is the number of completion and I felt that was God's way of telling us that our time in that house was complete. It was now time to move on. But surprisingly, that was not the only sign we received. That night as we looked at the printout, we discussed the price of the House, which was already less than the house we looked at originally. But I stated if the house were just $20,000 less, that would make it more "doable" for us. The next day. (Exactly seven years to the date that we had moved into the house we were living in at the time.) We went in to talk to the salesperson about what would ultimately become our home. Once we told the salesperson which house we were interested in, he, with no prompting, discussion, or haggling, told us that he would take $20,000 off the price of the House. Now you may not think that was a sign, but I felt in my heart that it was. I believe God gave us those signs to let us know from the start, that no matter what obstacles or hindrances came our way, he had already given us this house and we just needed to trust him through the process. And I tell you, it took a lot of trust. Even though we started with those two confirming signs, the path to the home was not paved. No, it was more like going off roading. There were rocks, holes, roots and one or two whole trees in our way. But despite all that, he was faithful and true to what I felt he had revealed. The most interesting part is that whenever something came up that made it seem like we were not going to be able to close on the home. And believe me, there were quite a few times that happened. I would still worry or cry, and on one or two occasions, I remember worrying and crying at the same time. Despite receiving those two signs of confirmation, my immediate response was to demonstrate my human frailty. Thankfully, I did not stay there too long. After a little bit of time, I would talk to God and myself. Telling him that I knew that this House was a part of his plan for us. And that I knew he hadn't brought us through all the other things to get us to that point and say, that's enough, you can't go any further. I would then remind myself that his promises are yes and Amen as it says in 2 Corinthians 1: 20. I reminded myself that he had already told me and my husband that this was our house. After doing all that, I would calm back down so that he could instruct me what to do in the natural as he worked all things out in the spiritual. Boy, when I tell you he showed out, he really showed out. Time, and time again. After being in this House for some time now, I still sit in awe of him and all he did to bless us with this home. I am also so incredibly grateful for all the people who were obedient to his promptings and allowed him to use them as vessels to bless us.

LISTENING

The final way to communicate that I will discuss is listening. You may recall back in chapter one, when I gave the definition for a source of information. In that explanation, I stated that I had to find real, factual, trustworthy authorities from whom to get my information. Which is why I use the Mayo Clinic for information about Health, Merriam Webster for my definitions, and Encyclopedia Britannica to learn about all things' trees. I could not just find some random and obscure website or book that said what I wanted to hear. I needed the truth backed up by evidence from a reputable source. I say all this because we should use the same criteria when determining who we listen to and allow to speak over us spiritually. My grandmother has a quote from one of her friends that she always says. "Speak spiritual things to spiritual people" and I am sure she wouldn't have a problem with me adding a little to it by saying, only listen to spiritual things from spiritual people.

Sometimes God tells other people things about you, and he allows them to share it with you. It may be a leader in the church, friends, or even family. But everyone that comes up to you telling you God told me to tell you... didn't get that information from God. Some people just name drop to get you to do something they want you to do or think you should do. I mentioned my friend Keisha earlier in this book. I have known her for almost 10 years now. When we first met, my youngest daughter was a baby, and I told her that I was not having any more kids. She laughed at me and told me that I was indeed going to have one more and that it would be a boy. I chuckled and shrugged it off. You see, I did not know her then, like I know her now. But every now and then she would remind me of that conversation. So, after about two or three years passed, I did get pregnant again and she was one of the first people I told. She laughed and said I knew it and it's going to be a boy. Indeed, it was a boy. Since then, there have been other times that she has shared things God placed on her heart with me. Needless to say, I no longer chuckle or shrugged them off. Not just because she got that one thing right, but because I have come to know her, and I see that she has a belief in God that is real and true. I have had the opportunity to be a firsthand eyewitness to her walk with the Lord. I see she has a trusting relationship with the father. She has proven herself to be a reliable source. So therefore, I have no problem listening when she speaks.

Listening is not just reserved for friends, relatives or in some instances, strangers on the street. We also have the opportunity to listen to our Pastors, Ministers, or Bible study leaders. Have you ever listened to a message and wondered if the speaker had cameras in your house because it seemed like he or she was speaking directly into your situation? I know I have. I believe on those occasions God is trying to get our attention. When I look back at those instances, I see that he may have used that message to confirm something he already put in my spirit. Or he used the message as a jumping off point and uses other things in my life throughout the week, month, day, or year as confirmation of that message.

However, the fact that they stand behind a podium, have a lot of followers, or have a title before their name doesn't qualify them to Minister to you. Before you start to follow anyone, whether that is to church or online, you must vet them. Ask yourself these three things:

1. **Is what they are saying biblically sound?** In order to know this, you must study the word for yourself. Our leaders are there to add to our knowledge of God, not to be the complete source of it. Nothing they teach should go against what the Bible tells us. There should be no contradiction to God's word.

2. **Does what they are saying about God line up with his character?** We know that God is good, and God is love. So, if they are teaching that he is anything but that. It goes against his character. We also know from James 1:17 that God does not change. Change occurs when there is a need to redirect or correct because of a mistake. But God does not make mistakes therefore there is no need for him to change.

3. **Is their life consistent with what they are saying?** Are they teaching and speaking about God, but you see no evidence of him in their lives or their interactions with others?

If the answer to any of these questions is no, then you may want to rethink allowing them to spiritually pour into you. I'm not telling you to judge other people, I'm telling you to vet the person or persons you are allowing to lead and/or teach you. Vetting is to thoroughly investigate someone or something before you decide to move forward with them. We were made to do life together and each of us are on different parts of our spiritual journey. Therefore, I don't want you to use these questions to determine every relationship in your life. I just want you to use it when determining how much spiritual weight you will give a person in a leadership position in your life. In Proverbs 27:17 it tells us that iron sharpens iron, which leads me to believe that sometimes we will be the ones getting sharpened and sometimes we will be the ones doing the sharpening. There are always going to be people in our lives that are more seasoned in their faith than us, as well as those that are newer in their faith than us. No matter where you fall, we are all a part of the community of believers.

Questions

1. What does John 10:27 tell us about our relationship with God?

2. Have you ever prayed continuously, like the example in the text? If not, I encourage you to try it and come back and answer the next part of this question. If so, do you feel it makes a difference in your day? Explain.

3. Based on the information in the text do you feel you are open to hearing from God either verbally, non-verbally, or through visual cues

4. What is the most common way you feel God communicates with you? Is there another way you would like to experience His communication?

5. What does each of the following verses say about how God feels about us? Do you believe it? Is it hard for you to believe it?

   a. John 3:16

   b. Psalms 103:12

   c. Isaiah 43:4

6. Based on Proverbs 27:17 List one person in your life that sharpens you, and one person you sharpen.

7. What is one thing that stood out to you the most in this chapter? Why do you feel God may want to point your attention to that?

Chapter Notes

CHAPTER 7 PART 2

THE COMMUNITY
OF BELIEVERS

While doing my research into all things fruit trees. I came across two words, Self-fruitful and self-unfruitful. I had no idea what either of these words truly meant. To begin to understand them, I had to first understand pollination. Pollination is when a pollinator like a bee takes pollen from the male part of a flower and then distributes it to the female part of a flower. This fertilizes the flower, and it will later yield fruit. Self-fruitful trees can pollinate themselves, meaning pollen from another flower on the same tree can be used in fertilization, or in some instances pollen from the same flower on the same tree can be used to fertilize itself, thus resulting in fruit growth. The flowers on self-unfruitful trees, however, cannot be fertilized from their own pollen. They need pollen from a different flower on a different tree to produce fruit. This brings me to the second and final perk I am going to cover. The community of believers.

I would like to use self-unfruitful trees as an analogy for us as Christians. We were created for fellowship, relationship, and companionship. God wants to have a relationship with us, and he wants us to have one with each other as well. He knew this was important from the beginning when he said in Genesis 2:18 it's not good for the man to be alone. Do not misunderstand me. I truly do believe that time spent alone is beneficial. You can use this time to pray, read, meditate, do devotions, or just to decompress. I don't think I ever really cherished my alone time any other time in my life as much as I did after having my children. My oldest is 14 years old and she will still come and stand on the outside of the bathroom door and talk to me while I am showering or otherwise engaged. So, I definitely know that alone time is needed. But as humans we are naturally social beings, and that doesn't change just because we have found God. Our relationship with God is a benefit to, not a replacement for, interpersonal relationships. According to psychologist John Cacioppo from the University of Chicago. Spending too much time alone can make you feel more stress and anxiety, raise your blood pressure, lead to poor sleep quality, as well as depression. Ecclesiastics 4: 12 uses rope as an analogy for friendship. Telling us that a 3-strand rope is not easily broken, which is a way of letting us know that we are stronger together. Some of us attempt to walk out our Christian journey like self-fruitful trees. We try to produce pollen, distribute the pollen, receive the pollen, and grow the fruit with no outside help. However, like I quoted before, Proverbs 27: 17 tells us that iron sharpens iron, which means, like the song says, I need you. You need me. We're all a part of God's body.

Christian friends can become like family really quickly. They can rejoice with you, cry with you, pray with you, and encourage you. I've been blessed to have many sisters in Christ in my life. Some I found through our kids being friends. Some I found at a Bible study or women's conference. Some I have known since my youth, and all parts of life in between. These women are the ones I call or text when I need someone to stand in the gap with and for me. I have also come to find that God will place them on my mind or me on theirs at just the right time. I can't tell you how many times I have called one of my sisters in Christ just because God had placed them on my heart. Only to find during our conversation that they are dealing with an issue or concern that God either wants me to help them with or pray and encourage them through. The same thing has happened to me. I will be struggling with something, and the phone will ring. A familiar voice on the other end will say something like; God just placed you on my heart and I wanted to reach out and check on you. That is the power of the community of believers. God will use others to bless you, and he will use you to bless others as well.

I think when we first start to prioritize God as our source, we can be guilty of retreating into our own little Godly bubble. When we find ourselves in this situation, we should not just decide to sit at home listening to gospel music, watching TBN every day. We must be open and get connected. If you are not a part of a body of believers, find one that you feel comfortable, welcome, and at home, then join it. This may take a few tries. Church is not one size fits all, if it were, there would not be so many of them. Once you have a church home, join a small group and volunteer in the church in some capacity. This is how you will start to find your people, build your community. Just know they may not look like you, act like you, or have the same life experiences as you. But trust me, none of that will matter. I know when I started to really pursue a relationship with God, it changed where I was comfortable going and what I was comfortable doing. My desires just were not the same. The people around me had to get accustomed to it, but I also had to give them an opportunity to do so.

Just because you have started to cultivate yourself a friend group of Christian believers, you can't cut all the ties to your existing friends. Now, don't get me wrong, if these friendships were hurtful or detrimental to your physical, emotional, or spiritual well-being, then cut away. But if that is not the case, remember what I said about us all being at different stages of our Christian walk. You may be called to sharpen some of those friends and introduce them to God as their source by them watching you live your life with him as yours. Remember, I said as Christians we are self-unfruitful trees. There is no way we can grow into who God created us to be, nor produce the fruit he created us to produce all on our own.

One of the most surprising things I have learned on this Christian journey is once you have an intimate relationship with God where you trust, believe, and have confidence in who he is, a lot of the things he does in your life are no longer only for your benefit. It is for the benefit of others. It is for those he places in your orbit that he is going to use you to disciple and/or bless. Do you get some residual blessings from it? Most of the time, yes. I like to use the example of transferring liquid from one container to another to illustrate this. Whenever I am getting water or juice for my husband or kids and it's the last of it. There are always some little droplets of water left in the empty container. The first container was just a means by which to transfer the liquid. But even though some liquid remains, the majority of it ends up in its intended container. This always reminds me of God and how, when he uses us, there's always residual blessings left in us. Though we are vessels being used by God, we are still his children. He is still growing, maturing, and strengthening us. So, a lot of times being used by him in the life of someone else will draw us closer to him ourselves and strengthen our relationship and confidence in him.

Life is hard, but life as a Christ follower is even harder because we were not created to be of this world. And we are constantly under attack from the devil that roams around, seeking whom he may devour, as it says in 1 Peter 5:8. That is why we are called to carry each other's burdens, help each other out Galatians 6:2. When we are aware of a struggle, we can and should pray for that person. But sometimes God will put you in a position to do more. Sometimes he will allow us to be the answer to the prayers, not just to pray them. I truly believe we are to be the hands and feet of God, with Jesus as our example to follow. And in Matthew 14:16 he speaks to all of us when he tells his disciples "You give them something to eat". He is telling them you are aware of the need. So instead of sending them away with that need unmet, trust me and as I supply, be obedient and watch me bless the multitude through you. Because of the obedience of the disciples, the people were fed. Because they were willing to put what they had in God's hands and allow Him to do with it as he pleased. The people were blessed. I believe the disciples benefited from this blessing as well. Yes, they did get to eat also. But even more so, seeing Him work in this way had to have increased their faith in Jesus. And I am sure it was that increase in faith that gave Peter the confidence to get out of the boat a few verses later. The fact that the God and creator of the Universe uses me to accomplish his plans, is amazing. What is even more amazing is what being used by him to bless others does for me and my faith and trust in Him. But it is not a one-way street. Just like he uses us to bless others, he will use others to bless us as well.

No matter where we find ourselves on this journey, we can all use some help or even just some encouragement. Hebrews 3:13 tells us to encourage one another daily. I do not know about you, but there are days when I am just down in the dumps. It's usually when I'm feeling like Paul in Romans 7:18-19. When I am not being who I know God created me to be. Having friends to come alongside me during those times and remind me of God's Grace, mercy, and most of all his unconditional love is definitely a perk.

Having someone to talk with about my struggles and pain is invaluable. James 5:16 tells us to confess our sins to each other and pray for each other so that we may be healed. If there is something you are struggling to get past, it's good to have someone there to talk with about it who will hold you accountable and help you get through it. It's always good to be the person that someone can confide in and share their struggles with. However, when we step into that role, we have to make sure we follow the directives set out in Romans 14:13. If people come to us and feel judged, they won't come again. We shouldn't judge others and we shouldn't do anything that would hinder someone's faith. We should be for others, the type of person we would like in our corner. Someone to intercede on our behalf when we need it. Now it tells you right there in James 5:16 that this person can't be just any old body. This person should be righteous. Simply put, the person should be in a right relationship with God. Why? Because that person, someone who is righteous, their prayers are powerful and effective. I don't know about you, but that is the person I want in my corner praying for me.

We shouldn't feel ashamed when we struggle because it tells us in 1 Peter 5:9 that the family of believers all over the world is dealing with the same kinds of suffering. That is why it's so important that we spur one another on toward love and good deeds, as it says in Hebrews 10:24. Having a support system or someone who is in your corner may sometimes mean the difference between being on a lifelong journey with the Lord and just taking him out for a spin. It's hard if there is no one there to pray with and for you, or to let you know that there is a way through whatever you are struggling with. Sometimes just hearing how God made a way where there seemed to be no way in someone else's life, makes all the difference in the world. Without that testimony or encouragement, the hard times can seem so unbearable that you just want to give up.

We each have a testimony and it is just what someone needs to hear. Our testimony might mean little to everyone, but it can mean everything to someone. Therefore, we should not be ashamed to share it when the time comes. Sometimes the way to get someone to allow you to help them carry their load is to let them know you have had a few of your own to carry. It can also be encouraging to hear how God brought you out of you circumstances, as well as what he taught you through it, and what he revealed to you after. My granny always tells me a quote her grandmother used to tell her. "Don't go through nothing you don't learn something from baby." Which just means there is a lesson in everything you go through. Make sure you learn it and as Christ followers we should also make sure we share it. And by sharing it, that's how we do what it tells us in Romans 14:19. Help each other have a strong faith (CEV).

Questions

1. *Has there ever been a time that you would have considered yourself to be attempting to be self-fruitful? If it has changed, what caused that change?*

2. *What are all the advantages of interpersonal relationships listed in Ecclesiastics 4: 9-12?*

3. *Read Matthew 14:13-21. Has there ever been a time when you felt God telling you to "give them something to eat"? In other words, God wanted to use you as the answer to someone else's prayer. Did you obey His calling?*

4. *Read, Romans 7:18-19. Have you ever felt like this? What did you do to get past it? Was there a friend who came alongside you to help and/ or encourage you during that time?*

5. *Read, Romans 14:13. What does it mean when it says, "do not put a stumbling block or obstacle in the way of your brother or sister."*

6. *Have you ever felt judged by a fellow brother or sister in Christ? What was the result?*

7. *What does 1 John 3:23 and Acts 2:46 tell us?*

Chapter Notes

NOTES

All Scripture is from the New International Version unless otherwise noted in the text

All definitions are from Merriam-Webster https://www.merriam-webster.com

All facts related to trees, water, and vines are from http://www.encyclopedia.com unless noted in the text

History of the French Language http://www.rosettastone.eu>french

The Bible App Videos Eyewitness Bible Series Vine, Branches, Fruit and Leaves: The Book of John

What is Spring? http://www.mysuwanneeriver.com/56/what-is-a-spring, Jan 25, 2019

Water: How much should you drink every day? http://www.mayoclinic.org>water By: Mayo Clinic Staff

The top 10 Reasons water is important http://www.theimportantsite.com

Pruning Bible App videos Nona Jones John 15:2

Effects of Water-borne disease and its prevention http://narayanahealth.org By: Dr. Joozer Rangwala

Grapevine Support Structure www.gardeningknowhow.com Supporting A Grapevine- How to make a Grapevine Support By: Amy Grant

5.2 Crown Classes- Forest Measurements http://openoregon.pressbooks. pub By: Joan DeYoung

Graft| Description, Types, & Uses http://www,britannica.com>topic By: The Editors of Encyclopedia Britannica

Trees Made Stronger by Bending in the Wind -UCCE Ventura County http://ceventura.ucanr.edu>Coastal

Printed in the United States
by Baker & Taylor Publisher Services